A Pilgrim's Journey

A Pilgrim's Journey

James Barrett

To order additional copies of this book, contact:
Xlibris Corporation
1-888-795-4274
www.Xlibris.com
Orders@Xlibris.com
86155

Contents

Dedication

I dedicate this book, "A Pilgrim's Journey," to my Mother, Margaret O'Neil Barrett, and to my Father, John Barrett. My parents had me baptized as a wee tiny baby, gave me a rock-solid Catholic education and taught me the fundamentals of my Faith. It was my Father and Mother who set me on the right path for my Life Journey.

Thank you, Mom. Thank you, Dad.

Author's Note

This book is a search for Truth. Is there or isn't there a God that created the Universe? That is the question. The book is rich in Evidence and Facts, Scientific Facts, to answer that question.

As a practicing Attorney, I spent 28 years evaluating Facts and Evidence; separating the wheat from the chaff, so to speak, as to what was true and what was false, erroneous or mistaken. I have set forth what I believe is the preponderance of the Evidence to support the Truth of the conclusions put forth in this book.

This then is my opinion and my solid belief and that is why I wrote this book. So right from the get-go, I ask that—"You be the Judge," to reach your own conclusions about the Life and Death issues set forth in the book.

I ask only that you ask yourself three questions:

Question #1   What do I believe?
Question #2   What is the evidence, the proof, the foundation for my belief?
Question #3   What happens when I die?

A Fellow Pilgrim

First Reviews

Reverend Robert J. Cook, President, Wyoming Catholic College

"A Pilgrim's Journey is the thought provoking testimony of a soul who has faithfully followed "the Way, the Truth and the Life" of his Lord, Jesus Christ. True to the Gospel, Jim Barrett shares for our benefit his profound insights into the great and central mysteries of life, from why we are here to where we are going. Central to this *Journey* is Barrett's belief in a God who in love created us, gives us a faith to be illumined by reason and certified by our conscience, and wants nothing more than to redeem us. Barrett spells out what is needed for a life of purpose and meaning. The author offers a challenging and transcendent vision from his personal *Journey* through life seeking to the only goal that makes any sense, eternal life in love with a Trinitarian God. For those who truly want to think about the realities of life in profound ways, this book is an ideal read."

Curtis Martin, Founder & President of the Fellowship of Catholic University Students (FOCUS)

"A Pilgrim's Journey is a great reminder of how we ought to think . . . about everything. Jim Barrett does us a great favor by helping us to look at reality in an honest way. The ancients used to refer to creation as the first book of divine revelation; years of influence from secular humanism and atheism may have dulled our senses but this book refocuses our

vision so that we can see what the Scriptures declare. "The heavens are telling the glory of God and the firmament proclaims his handiwork." (Psalm 19:1)

Introduction

A friend once observed that any argument, no matter how intelligent or foolish, seems to have more gravity when the person making it wears a white lab coat. And it's true: The more we clothe an opinion or a product in the liturgical vestments of "science," the more likely people will be to accept it. In a sense, in the minds of many people today, the white lab coat often works like a new kind of Roman collar. It's the uniform of a new secular clergy.

Science of course has given us many extraordinary gifts. But it has not, and never will, solve the problem of our mortality. Nor can it give us ultimate answers about why we exist, the purpose of our lives or what comes after death. Our very human habit of asking these basic questions about meaning—questions that flow naturally from the deepest recesses of the heart—cannot be shrugged off as a genetic curiosity of the human animal. The great Catholic scientist Blaise Pascal reminded us that the heart has its reasons that reason cannot know. Men and women are more than their biochemistry or the electrical activity in their brains. Denying the reality of the spirit, that intimate and unique personal essence Christians call the soul, is simply another form of inhumanity kidnapping science as an alibi for unbelief.

The genius of Christianity is that it speaks with equal power to the rich and the poor; the brilliant and the lowly. It answers our most urgent questions about life in profoundly challenging ways. The Gospel is for every man and woman in every age, and each pilgrim on the road to heaven has something uniquely valuable to share with every other pilgrim.

So it is with this small but engaging volume. Jim Barrett makes no claim that A Pilgrim's Journey is a "grand" book or that it answers every urgent question about God, faith and unbelief. But he speaks with the kind of clarity, zeal and uncommon common sense that comes from great experience on the road of discipleship. And therein lies its value as a source of solace and confidence.

+Charles J. Chaput, O.F.M. Cap.
Archbishop of Denver

Preface

This is an amazing country we live in—majestic mountains, gorgeous rivers, stark deserts, rippling plains of bountiful wheat and corn; a land with two spectacular oceans, the Pacific and the Atlantic.

It's dramatic, beautiful and full of wondrous places. This book is about our world and our life. I write it as a Pilgrim on Life's Journey in the hope of helping my fellow Pilgrims to understand the Reality of Creation—the Universe, the World, and all that is alive in that Creation, including you and me. Every Human Being is mortal; his life has a beginning, a living and a death; all that is mortal becomes, "Finito." It then clearly is in the category of a journey for each of us.

I remember several trips (journeys) I took and the excitement of heading for the mountains, the desert, the Colorado river. These were instantly forgotten on the trip because of a flat tire, or when the engine of the motor home I was driving caught on fire or running out of gas late in the day 40 miles away from the nearest gas station while traveling across the high desert (to name but a few; I'm sure you've had your own mini-disasters).

I tell this personal anecdote because of the "Good Sams" I met—total strangers who came to my rescue. (Do you remember the "Good Sam" logo you'd see on campers and trailers of fellow travelers? Thousands of them! Good people—ready to help anyone at anytime.)

Well, this book is written by me as a "Good Sam," to get you thinking about the good roads for your trip through life; mileage markers to tell you where you are at some point in your journey and to help you figure out your Final Destination. I wish you a safe journey . . .

A Fellow Pilgrim,

Jim Burrett

Prelude

Thinking about Thinking

In the act of Thinking, there is Hierarchy. The Hierarchy is this:

At the 1st Level–   Knowledge

At the 2nd Level–   Understanding

And, at the top . . .
       3rd Level–   Wisdom

1st Level–Knowledge

Man is a "Seeker"–He uses the four powers of his mind:
    Intellect * Memory * Imagination * and, the Will (To Act)

2nd Level–Understanding

In Physics–we seek to understand physical things and laws. We learn about the Physical World.

In Biology–we seek to understand Life's processes—Birth, Growth and Death of all living things.

In Spirituality–we seek to understand the meaning, the purpose of Life. The key word here is Understanding. What is the Significance of this Knowledge?

3rd Level–Wisdom

And now we come to the pinnacle of thinking . . . Wisdom. The use of the powers of our mind and our experience to seek Truth, Beauty and Goodness in all of Creation.

Every person seeks to know so he seeks Information. From this Information, each person makes decisions; he then forms conclusions which become his Beliefs.

This all takes place in the mind and become fixed as his personal Beliefs. Whether his Beliefs are in conformity with the Facts, the Truth, the Reality, is another matter entirely. Objective Facts trump opinions every time if personal opinion is not in agreement with objective Reality (i.e., the Truth of the matter); regardless of whether that opinion is held by one person or millions of people.

Chapter #1

Creation of the Universe

"The world was made, not in time, but simultaneous with time. For that which is made in time is made both after and before some time–after that which is past, before that which is future. But none could then be past, for there was no creature whose movements its duration could be measured. But simultaneously with time the world was made." (St. Augustine said this–in the 4ᵗʰ Century!)

"In the beginning, God made the Heavens and the Earth and said, 'Let there be Light.' The First Day." (This is an exact quote from the Bible-Genesis).

Does Scientific evidence support or discredit this Creation story? Let's look at what Science has discovered. It is astounding–it really does matter, and matter very much, how we think about the Cosmos. Our concept of the Universe shapes our world view, our Philosophy of Life, and thus our daily decisions and actions. If the Universe was not created and "just happened," meaning, and consequently, life, including human life, has no meaning. If the Universe is created, then there must be a Creator who exists outside of His Creation. Nothing "just happens."

Atoms, rocks, flowers, creatures exist. When and how did this happen?
Let's look at the Facts . . . the Evidence.

To study the origin and development of the Universe is, in a sense, to
investigate the basis for any meaning and purpose to life. Cosmology
has deep theological and philosophical ramifications.

Many researchers refuse to acknowledge this connection. They gather
and examine data through a special pair of glasses, the "God-is-not-
necessary-to-explain-anything" glasses. It's tough for them to admit that
such lenses represent their theological position, their personal faith.

Our galaxy contains a hundred billion suns and our Universe holds
more than a hundred billion galaxies. The immensity of it. A sense
of awe concerning nature. Its beauty and harmony, combined with its
staggering complexity—who or what could be responsible for it all? If
the Universe arose out of a Big Bang, it must have had a beginning. If it
had a beginning, it must have a Beginner. That Beginner was God. Who
says so? God says so. On the first day of Creation He said, "Let there
be light." Thousands of years later, Science has conclusive proof that
was exactly what happened–an explosion of immense light and energy
which we call . . . the "Big Bang." Awesome . . .

The first chapter of the Bible is a journal-like record of the earth's initial
conditions—correctly described from the standpoint of astrophysics
and geophysics—followed by a summary of the sequence of changes
through which Earth came to be inhabited by living things and ultimately
by humans. The account was simple, the order and the description of
creation events perfectly matched the established record of nature.

The Scientific search began about 100 years ago to find out if there was any evidence to show that the Universe had a beginning. In the 18th century, Scientists observed Entropy—a measurement of a loss of energy in the Universe and stated—the Second Law of Thermodynamics—which is still one of the most fundamental Laws of Physics.

In the 1930's—Albert Einstein published his theory of General Relativity. Mathematician Willen de Sitter then found a solution to Einstein's equations as predicting an expanding Universe.

In the 1920's, Einstein's theory was further confirmed by Astronomer, Edwin Hubble. He observed a "Red Shift" in serial observations which proved that planets and galaxies were hurtling away from one another at fantastic speeds. Space itself was expanding!

Astronomy is the oldest numerical Science, crucial in ancient times for calendars and navigation. It is now experiencing a surge of discovery. The enhanced focus on time as we enter the new millennium is boosting interest in our cosmic environment. Astronomy is still the Science of numbers; there are <u>six numbers</u> that are crucial for the creation of the Universe, and our place in it.

<u>On the blurred boundaries of ancient maps, cartographers wrote, "There be dragons</u>." After the pioneer navigators had encircled the globe and delineated the main continents and oceans, later explorers filled in the details. But there was no longer any hope of finding a new continent, or any expectation that the Earth's size and shape would ever be drastically reappraised.

At the end of the twentieth century we have, remarkably, reached the same stage in mapping our Universe: the grand outlines are now coming into focus. This is the collective achievement of thousands of astronomers, physicists and engineers, using many different techniques. Modern telescopes probe deep into space; because the light from distant objects takes a long time journeying towards us, they also give us glimpses of the remote past; we have detected 'fossils' laid down in the first few seconds of cosmic history. Spacecraft have revealed neutron stars, black holes, and other extreme phenomena that extend our knowledge of the physical laws. These advances have vastly stretched our cosmic horizons. There has, in parallel, been an exploration of the micro world within the atom, yielding new insights in to the nature of space on the tiniest of scales.

The picture that emerges–a map in time as well as in space–is not what most of us expected. It offers a new perspective on how a single 'genesis event' created billions of galaxies, black holes, stars and planets, and how atoms have been assembled–here on Earth, and perhaps on other worlds—into living beings intricate enough to ponder their origins. There are deep connections between stars and atoms, between the cosmos and the micro world. There is a book entitled, "*Just Six Numbers*," by Martin Rees. This book describes–without technicalities–the forces that control us and, indeed, our entire Universe. Two are basic forces–"*N*" and "*E*". Two fix the size and texture of the Universe—"Ω" and "λ". Two fix the properties of Space—"*Q*" and "*D*".

N—a number measuring the strength of the electrical forces holding atoms together divided by the force of Gravity between them.

"*E*"—defines how atomic nuclei bind together and how atoms on Earth were made.

"Ω"—measures the amount of material in the Universe. It defines the importance of Gravity and expansion energy.

"λ"—"Cosmic anti-Gravity." This caused stars to form and started the Cosmic evolution.

"*Q*"—Measures two fundamental energies in the "Big Bang" which formed the stars and galaxies.

"*D*"—Defines Space and Time.

* * *

On April 24, 1992, a team of Astrophysicists had reported from the Cosmic Background Recorder (COBE) stunning confirmation of the hot Big Bang creation event. The COBE satellite was designed specifically to find the explanation of how galaxies form out of a Big Bang. Professor of Mathematics, Stephen Hawking, said: "It is the discovery of the century, if not of all time." Michael Turner, Astrophysicist with the University of Chicago, and Fermilab, termed the discovery "unbelievably important . . . the significance of this cannot be overstated." "What we have found is evidence for the birth of the Universe." He added, "It is like looking at God."

These new results do more than just prove that the Universe began with a hot Big Bang. They tell us which kind of hot Big Bang it was.

The hot Big Bang model says that the entire physical Universe—all the matter and energy, and even the four dimensions of space and time—burst forth from a state of infinite, or near infinite, density, temperature, and pressure. The Universe expanded from a volume.

The cumulative evidence from the Hubble and the COBE tests helped solve the mystery of how galaxies and clusters of galaxies form out of a hot Big Bang creation event.

Actually, a model of the Universe was developed as a <u>Theory</u> and many of its basic components were predicted by Physicists working in the early part of the twentieth century. Richard Tolman in 1922 recognized that since the Universe is expanding, it must be cooling off from an exceptionally high initial temperature. The laws of thermodynamics say that any expanding system must be cooling simultaneously. George Gamow in 1946 discovered that only a rapid cooling of the cosmos from near infinitely high temperatures could account for how protons and neutrons fused together, forming a Universe that today is about 73% hydrogen, 24% helium, and 3% heavier elements.

Also, concurrently an instrument measured, by radio wavelengths, the cosmic background radiation (i.e., heat) to be about 3° centigrade above absolute zero. Only a hot Big Bang could account for such a huge specific entropy for the Universe. It was demonstrated, further, that if the specific entropy were any greater or any less, stars and planets could never have formed at all.

Ordinary matter is the stuff we are used to—matter made up of protons, neutrons, electrons, and other fundamental particles. Such matter strongly interacts with radiation. Exotic matter has the opposite characteristic; it does not strongly interact with radiation.

In 1905, Albert Einstein published his initial theory of special relativity; it focused only on velocity. Results, published in 1915 and 1916, were the equations of general relativity, equations that carry profound implications about the nature and origin of the Universe.

These equations show that the Universe is simultaneously expanding and decelerating. What phenomenon behaves this way? There is one: an explosion. Astronomer Edwin Hubble (1889-1953) in 1929 proved from his measurements on forty different galaxies that the galaxies indeed are expanding away from one another. Moreover, he demonstrated that expansion was in the same manner predicted by Einstein's original formulation of general relativity. Einstein acknowledged "the necessity for a beginning" and "the presence of a superior reasoning power."

In the Physical Sciences, Evolution typically is defined as change taking place with respect to time. The Bible is "evolutionary" in its teachings on creation since it frames the creation account into a chronology of change through time–eleven major creation events sequenced over six creation days.

The space-time theorem presented by Astronomer Stephen Hawking and fellow Scientists Penrose and Ellis, are based on solid conclusive evidence. This space-time theorem tells us that the dimensions of length, width, height, and time have existed only for as long as the Universe has been expanding. Time really does have a beginning.

Time is that dimension in which cause-and-effect phenomena take place. No time, no cause and effect. If time's beginning is concurrent with the beginning of the Universe, as the space-time theorem says, then the cause of the Universe must be some entity operating in the time dimension of the Universe. This conclusion is powerfully important to our understanding of who God is and who or what God isn't. It tells us that the Creator is transcendent, operating beyond the dimensional limits of the Universe. It tells us that God is not the Universe itself, nor is God contained within the Universe.

All the data accumulated in the twentieth century tells us that a transcendent Creator must exist, for all the matter, energy, length, width, height, and even time itself suddenly and simultaneously came into being from a source beyond itself. Science leads us to these conclusions, but so also does the Bible, and it is the only holy book to do so.

> *Through him all things were made; without him nothing was made that has been made.*
>
> —(John 1:3)

> *For by him all things were created: things in heaven and on earth, visible and invisible, whether thrones or powers or rulers or authorities; all things were created by him and for him. He is before all things; and in him all things hold together.*
>
> —(Colossians 1:16-17)

This passage says that, in coming to Earth, Jesus Christ stripped Himself of the extra-dimensional capacities He shared with God the Father and the Holy Spirit. These capacities were restored to Him once He had fulfilled His mission of redeeming Human Beings from their sin.

There is now a frustrated and defiant reaction by Secular Humanists to mounting evidence from physics and astronomy that the Universe–all matter, energy, space and time–began in a Creation Event, and that the Universe was specifically designed for life. Obviously, this unexpected turn of events producing solid Scientific research proves discouraging to those who are hostile to the message of salvation in Jesus Christ. Researchers are groping for a substitute replacement; an "Anything But Theory" in place of the overwhelming Scientific evidence of how the Universe was created.

As every student of philosophy knows, anything can be speculated by using our Imagination. "Ockham's Razor," is a guiding principle of Western Science; it states that the most plausible explanation is that which contains the simplest ideas and fewest assumptions—and that is the clear factual evidence of the Scientific proof of the "Big Bang."

Professor Davies, in a book published in 1984, wrote that the laws of physics "seem themselves to be the product of exceedingly ingenious design."

The Expansion of the Universe

The first parameter of the Universe to be measured was the Universe's expansion rate. If the Universe expanded too rapidly, none of it would clump enough to form galaxies. If no galaxies form, no stars will form. If no stars form, no planets will form. If no planets form, there's no place for life. The second parameter of the Universe to be measured was its age. A third parameter is entropy, or energy degradation. A fourth parameter, another very sensitive one, is the ratio of the electromagnetic force constant to the gravitational force constant. The degree of fine tuning is utterly amazing.

God and the Astronomers

The discovery of this degree of design in the Universe is having a profound theological impact. Davies has moved from promoting atheism to conceding that "the laws of physics . . . seem themselves to be the product of exceedingly ingenious design." "There is powerful evidence . . . the impression of design is overwhelming."

Astronomer George Greenstein said, "As we survey the evidence, some supernatural agency–or rather, Agency–must be involved. The medieval theologian who gazed at the night sky through the eyes of Aristotle and saw angels moving the spheres in harmony has become the modern cosmologist who gazes at the same sky though the eyes of Einstein and see the hand of God not in angels but in the constants of nature. When confronted with the order and beauty of the Universe and the strange coincidences of nature, it's very tempting to take the leap of faith from science into religion. I am sure many physicists want to. I only wish they would admit it."

Cosmologists Bernard Carr and Martin Rees state, "Nature does exhibit remarkable coincidences and these do warrant some explanation. One would have to conclude either that the features of the Universe invoked in support of the Anthropic Principle are only coincidences or that the Universe was indeed tailor-made for life. I will leave it to the theologians to ascertain the identity of the tailor!"

Physicist Freeman Dyson: "The problem here is to try to formulate the ultimate purpose of the Universe." Vera Kistiakowsky, MIT physicist: "The exquisite order displayed by our scientific understanding of the physical world calls for the divine." Anzo Penzias, who shared the Nobel prize for Physics remarked: "Astronomy leads us to a unique event, a Universe which was created out of nothing, one with the very delicate balance needed to provide exactly the conditions required to permit life, and one which has an underlying (one might say 'supernatural') plan."

Allan Sandage, winner of the Craafoord prize in Astronomy remarked: "I find it quite improbable that such order came out of chaos. God to me is a mystery but where is the explanation for the miracle of existence? Why is there something instead of nothing?"

Astrophysicist Robert Jastrow, a self-proclaimed Agnostic said: "For the scientist who has lived by his faith in the power of reason, the story ends like a bad dream. He has scaled the mountains of ignorance; he is about to conquer the highest peak; as he pulls himself over the final rock, he is greeted by a band of theologians who have been sitting there for centuries."

Not one person denies the conclusion that somehow the Universe has been crafted to make it a fit habitat for life. The evidence permits only two options: divine design or blind chance. Words such as *somebody fine tuned nature, superintellect, monkeyed, overwhelming design, hand of God, ultimate purpose, God's mind, exquisite order, very delicate balance, exceedingly ingenious, supernatural Agency, supernatural plan, tailor-made, Supreme Being,* and *providentially crafted* obviously apply to a Person.

When it comes to the causes, developmental processes, and origins, two possibilities exist: natural or supernatural. To dogmatically insist that supernatural answers must never be considered is equivalent to demanding that all human beings follow only one religion, the religion of atheistic materialism.

*   *   *

Our emergence and survival depend on very special 'tuning' of the Universe.

> *Who could believe an ant in theory?*
> *A giraffe in blueprint?*
> *Ten thousand doctors of what's possible*
> *Could reason half the jungle out of being.*

Gravity grips planets in their orbits and holds the stars together. Entire galaxies–swarms of billions of stars–are governed by Gravity. No substance, not even light itself, escapes its grasp. It controls the expansion of the entire Universe.

Gravity presents deep mysteries. Newton showed that the force holds the planets in their elliptical orbits around the Sun. Gravity acts on clusters of stars and, in galaxies, where billions of stars are held in orbit around a central hub.

In the Sun and other stars like it, there is a balance between Gravity, which pulls them together, and the pressure of their hot interior, which, if Gravity didn't act, would make them fly apart. In our own Earth's atmosphere, the pressure at ground level, likewise, balances the weight of all the air above us.

More than two centuries after Newton, <u>Einstein</u> proposed his theory of Gravity known as "<u>General Relativity</u>". According to this theory, planets actually follow the straightest path in a 'space-time' that is curved by the presence of the Sun. It is commonly claimed that Einstein 'overthrew' Newtonian physics, but this is misleading. Newton's law still describes motions in the Solar System with good precision. Einstein's theory, copes (unlike Newton's) with objects whose speeds are close to that of light, with the ultra-strong Gravity that could induce such enormous speeds, and with the effect of Gravity on light itself. Einstein showed that this was a path in space-time curved by mass and energy. The theory of General Relativity stemmed from Einstein's deep insight rather than specific experiment or observation. Genius!

The cumulative Scientific evidence and knowledge of the Universe has been amazing and startling. <u>In the 1990's, Astrophysicist Steven Weinberg, wrote a book called, "*The First Three Minutes*," which shook the Scientific community to its foundations. It is known by us as, "The Big Bang."</u> It stated that <u>the factual evidence was overwhelming that the Universe had a beginning fifteen billion years ago and . . . before that, there was Nothing! No Matter, no Space, no Time, Nothing.</u> Weinberg states: "<u>It was light</u> that formed the dominant constituent of the Universe." The energy explosion was massive. <u>The supporting evidence for proof of the "Big Bang" is overwhelming and conclusive and is now confirmed by Astronomers, Physicists and Mathematicians. The evidence to prove this is overwhelming.</u>

Light is energy–in the form of electricity and magnetism. The speed of light is 189,000 feet per second [it is absolute]. Scientists know of four forces: three that govern the Micro-World—Electro-Magnetism, the Nuclear Force, and the "Weak Force"; and one that governs the Macro-World–Gravity.

Before the Big Bang–there was no physical matter so there were no Laws of Physics. The Laws were not invented by Scientists; they discovered these "Laws"–and learned step by step how these Laws control and govern the myriad relationships and order of objects and living Beings in the World and the Universe.

Certain Scientists, who are Secular Humanists, tried to explain away the Big Bang–they theorized (with no evidence; no proof that the Universe was infinite in age and thus didn't have a beginning). It was called the "Steady State" Theory. The "Steady State" Theory, however, suffered a devastating blow when Bell Lab Scientists (radio engineers) discovered mysterious radiation coming from the Universe itself. NASA's cosmic background explorer satellite ("COBE") also confirmed that this radiation analysis proved without question that indeed the Universe was created out of nothing–15 billion years ago!!

What have the Secular Scientists had to say about who or what put all this astounding Matter and Energy in the Universe? Answer—"No one did. It 'just happened!!'" Science deals only with facts—what exists—this is all Science can do.

Scientists have encountered an absolute and impenetrable barrier; they can go no further. The bounds of our Universe are all they can know–there are no "Physics" and there is no "Time" or "Space" beyond the Universe.

The empirical support for a Big Bang fifteen billion years ago is as compelling as the evidence that geologists offer on our Earth's history. This is an astonishing turnaround. Everything in our observable Universe started as a compressed fireball, far hotter than the center of the Sun. Advances, observations and experiments have brought the broad cosmic picture of certainty to ninety-nine per cent.

The Laws of Physics that Einstein discovered apply not just here on Earth but also in the remotest galaxy. All parts of the Universe are seen to be evolving in a similar way.

Recent advances bring into focus new mysteries about the origin of our Universe, the laws governing it, and even its eventual fate. These pertain to the first tiny fraction of a second after the Big Bang, when conditions were so extreme that the relevant Physics isn't understood–we wonder about time, dimensions, the origin of matter, and the way the Cosmos and the Micro-World are intimately connected.

In Summary:

All the evidence of Science establishes that there was a Creation event 15 billion years ago; before that—there was no matter, no things, nothing. In short, it was created out of nothing and came into existence. The Universe was produced; this is a creative act; an intelligent act. Mind produced it; Matter cannot! It was Super-Natural (beyond Physics). Our World looks and feels so solid and material but now we know with Scientific certainty it was created by a force before and beyond Physics. It is called by Philosophers and Theologians–Metaphysics.

<u>Meta-physics is of the Spirit; not the Flesh, not of Matter.</u> Modern Science corroborates the Biblical creation story of 2500 B.C. (4,500 years ago) told to God's people, the Jews, by God of how He created the world. How about that!

The Mind of God is the origin of Matter. It is Mind that produces Matter not the other way around as the Atheists believe.

Is it reasonable for us to believe that the Act of Creation was done by God? Of course; every act has a cause; in this case God is the Cause. So says the Bible in Genesis, Chapter One and Modern Science has now confirmed the truth of the Biblical story. The findings of modern Physics, Astronomy, Biology and Mathematics provide powerful and convincing corroborative evidence of the existence of an eternal, Super-Natural Being who created the Universe and everything in it. We Christians call this Being–God, the Almighty Father.

Chapter #2

The Creation Story

What is Man's Place in the Universe?

Is Man just another species of animal—an Intelligent Ape—or is he something more than that? Reductionists and Behaviorists say Man is, "nothing but a Naked Ape". Skinner/Pavlov and Lorenz (all renowned Scientists) believed that Man is "nothing but" an intelligent animal; a "Naked Ape". Pavlov's dogs/ Skinner's rats/Lorenz's geese were examples to "prove" this. These Scientists were Atheists who believe Man has no purpose and Life has no meaning other than that of an animal who becomes extinct when its heart stops beating.

Are we created beings or a bunch of atoms that "just happened" to "get together", just happened to become "alive", just happened to start "thinking", just happened to know intuitively "right" from "wrong"? The "Easter Bunny" makes more sense!

Man is much, much more than just a thinking animal. Other animals think–my dog, Daisy, is a wondrous thinker in the world of dogs–but she is not a Human Being who has four powers of the Mind–Intellect, Memory, Imagination and Will. Man has these as part of the very core of his Being; in short, it is his Nature as a <u>Human</u> Being—and a very special Being he is.

It is a core belief of the major religions of the world—Judaism, Christianity and Islam—that Man has a privileged status and place in God's creation of the Universe. He created Man in <u>His own Image</u> and gave him dominion over all living creatures.

*   *   *

What we are focusing on now however is how we, in our day and age, understand what Man's place is in this vast Universe. Various and conflicting Theories have been proposed down through the Ages but today with the discoveries in Mathematics, Astronomy and related Scientific activities such as photography, nuclear laboratories and many, many specialized disciplines, startling and astonishing knowledge, facts and proofs about our Universe and Man's place in it are now known conclusively. The proof is before our very eyes!!

Scientists once thought they had positive proof that we Humans are not special because we live on a tiny, insignificant planet in one of billions of galaxies in a distant part of an unimaginably vast Universe. "There is no God," became the Mantra of Philosophers <u>and</u> Scientists. A small minority of Scientists believed the World was specially made for Humans; they called their Theory the "<u>Anthropic Principle</u>." They were laughed at and ridiculed by the Scientific Establishment.

The Scientific Establishment is not laughing now. The proof is overwhelming that they are wrong. All the various Scientific Disciplines corroborate each other that our World is a very, very special place, specially made for Man. Let's look at the Evidence and Facts.

Scientists studying the Big Bang have shown that the great age and vast size of the Universe are indispensable conditions for life on Earth. In other words, there would be no Human Beings without the creation of the Universe. This is where it gets very, very interesting.

Scientists have shown that six factors underlie the fundamental physical properties of the Universe and each must be of the precise value that it is or life could not occur. Not only that, all six factors must exist at the same time and in a precise sequence! The gravitational constant, the strong nuclear force, gravity, the proton mass, the electron charge–all interacting so as to create life on planet Earth.

To prove this point, here is a quote from Physicist Stephen Hawking–"If the rate of expansion one second after the Big Bang had been smaller by one part in a 100,000 million-million, the Universe would have re-collapsed and would not exist." The odds of our not being here would be astronomical–no Universe, no people, no you and me.

The Atheist belief is, "There is no God." Physicist Steven Weinberg writes, "The human race has had to grow up a good deal in the last five hundred years to confront the fact that we don't count for much in the grand scheme of things." Astronomer Carl Sagan invoked the Copernican revolution to challenge, "our posterings, our imagined self-importance, the delusion that we have some privileged position in the Universe." The Copernican revolution can be understood as establishing the principle of mediocrity. The principle simply says that we Human Beings are nothing special. We inhabit a tiny insignificant planet in a relatively undistinguished galaxy in a distant suburb of an unimaginably vast Universe. "<u>This is not Science! It is a person's belief!</u>" Unsupported in any way by Science.

In recent years, Physics has given this Atheist position a resounding "Not True" that overthrows the principle of mediocrity and affirms Man's special place in the cosmos. It turns out that the vast size and great age of our Universe are necessary. They are the indispensible conditions for the existence of life on Earth. In other words, the Universe has to be just as big as it is and just as old as it is in order to contain living inhabitants like you and me. Physicists call this incredible finding the <u>Anthropic Principle</u>, which states that the Universe we know must be of precisely such a nature as will make possible living beings who can perceive it. The entire Universe follows a very specific set of rules.

Consider the force of Gravity. Why is the Gravitational Force just this strong and not stronger or weaker? Consider that the Universe is approximately fifteen billion years old and at least fifteen billion light years in size. What would have happened if the Universe was much older and bigger or much younger and smaller?

In order for life to exist, the Scientific evidence is that the Gravitational Force had to be precisely what it is. <u>The Big Bang had to occur exactly when it did</u>. If the basic values and relationships of nature were even slightly different, our Universe would not exist and neither would we. Fantastic though it seems, the Universe is fine-tuned for human habitation. We live in a kind of Goldilock's Universe in which the conditions are "just right" for life to emerge and thrive. As Physicist Paul Davies puts it, "We have been written into the laws of nature in a deep and, I believe, meaningful way."

In Astronomer Martin Rees's book, *"Just Six Numbers,"* Rees shows that six numbers underlie the fundamental physical properties of the Universe, and that each must be an exact value required for life to exist. If any one of the six numbers (say the gravitational constant, or the strong nuclear force) were different "even to the tiniest degree," Rees says, "there would be no stars, no complex elements, no life." The mass of the proton, the charge of the electron, the gravitational constant are critical for life to exist.

Physicist Stephen Hawkings: "If the rate of expansion one second after the Big Bang had been smaller by even one part in a hundred thousand million-million, the Universe would have recollasped before it even reached its present size." The odds against us being here are, well, astronomical. And yet we are here.

St. Paul writes in his first letter to the Romans, that, "ever since the creation of the world, His invisible nature, namely His eternal power and deity, has been clearly perceived in the things that have been made." In the Anthropic Principle we seem to have a thrilling confirmation of these ancient passages. Not only does the Anthropic Principle suggest a Creator who is incomparably intelligent, but it also suggests a Creator who has special concern for us. This is a personal Creator, not some abstract "first mover."

Through Science we are witnessing powerful evidence that our human destiny is part of a Divine Plan. Contrary to the Principle of Mediocrity, we live in a meaningful and purposeful Universe. The Anthropic Principle gives powerful evidence for our belief that we Human Beings are part of the intended handiwork of a God who loves us.

Certain leading Scientists have acknowledged the far-reaching implications of the Anthropic Principle. "A commonsense interpretation of the facts," writes astronomer Fred Hoyle, "suggests that a super-intellect has monkeyed with the laws of physics." Physicist Freeman Dyson says, "The more I examine the Universe and study the details of its architecture, the more evidence I find that the Universe in some sense must have known we were coming."

Astronomer Owen Gingerich writes that the Anthropic Principle "means accepting that the laws of nature are rigged not only in favor of complexity or just in favor of life, but also in favor of mind. To put it dramatically, it implies that mind is written into the laws of nature in a fundamental way."

Astronomer Robert Jastrow observes that the Anthropic Principle "is the most theistic result ever to come out of science."

The Anthropic Principle has provoked a huge debate and strong reaction. In this debate there are three possible positions–1) "Lucky Us", 2) "Multiple Universes", and 3) "A Designed Universe".

"Lucky Us" attributes the fine-tuning of the Universe to incredible coincidences. In Science this is called a "selection effect." Since we are here, (we know that)–whatever the odds are–the game of cosmic chance must have worked out in our favor. **Taking all the known and proven evidence, Mathematicians give the odds of "Lucky Us" being correct as 100 billion to 1 against.** "Lucky Us"–it is day-dreaming.

The Anthropic Principle does not say that, given the billions of stars in the Universe, it's remarkable that life turned up on our planet. Rather, it says that the entire Universe with all the galaxies and stars in it had to be formed in a certain way in order for it to contain life at all. Philosopher Antony Flew, long a champion of Atheism, concluded that the fine-tuning of the Universe at every level is simply too perfect to be the result of chance. Flew says that in keeping with his lifelong commitment, "to go where the evidence leads," he now believes in God.

The second explanation for the Anthropic Principle is—"Multiple Universes." There are several versions of the Multiple Universes theory. One version is that the Big Bang spawned multiple universes, each with its own set of laws. Another is that our Universe emerged from a black hole in a previous Universe, and all the black holes in our Universe are even now generating other Universes. More day-dreaming by the "anything but God" gang.

What is one to make of all this? As with all Scientific theories, we begin by asking for the evidence. So where is the empirical evidence for oscillating and parallel and multiple Universes? There isn't any. Atheist Weinberg admits, "These are very speculative ideas . . . without any experimental support." Pure speculation–no Facts/no Evidence/no Scientific Proof . . . Nada!

Anyone who can believe in multiple Universes should have no problem believing in Heaven and Hell. Just think of them as alternate Universes, operating outside space and time according to laws that are inoperative in our Universe. Even the Atheist should now be able to envision a realm in which there is no evil or suffering and where the inhabitants never grow old. These traditional concepts, which have long been dismissed as preposterous based on the rules of our World, should be quite believable and perhaps even mandatory for one who holds that there are an infinite number of Universes in which all quantum possibilities are realized.

There is a principle of logic, widely accepted in science, called the principle of Occam's Razor. It means that when there are a variety of possible explanations, go with the one that requires the fewest assumptions. Applying Occam's Razor, Carl Sagan urges that "when faced with two hypotheses that explain the data equally well, choose the simpler." Biologist E.O. Wilson writes that the difficult thing about this principle for many people is that it "grants less license for New Age dreaming . . . but it gets the world straight."

There are multiple objections to all theories of multiple Universes. They invent a fantastically complicated set of circumstances to explain a single case when there is a much simpler, more obvious explanation right at hand. The Anthropic Principle says, quite simply, that our Universe is designed for life because someone designed it. The Designer Universe approach has this benefit: you don't need to make up the idea of a 100 billion Universes that you know nothing about in order to account for the only Universe we do know something about; the one we actually live in. Yet this third response seems to be anathema to some people and here we see how strongly modern Atheism relies on "New Age Dreaming". Rather than consider these theories Scientific, we need to label them as a Religious Doctrine. **Hawking, Weinberg, Dawkins, and the others are all members of the Church of the Infinite Worlds**. For members of this church, the dogmas seem to be largely motivated by the desire to avoid a Supernatural Creator.

It is pure speculation without a shred of Scientific Fact or Evidence to believe in imaginary time and multiple Universes; these are only concepts. Further, they do not explain <u>why</u> there is a Universe in the first place. Moreover, the Secular Humanist viewpoint cannot explain the profound lawfulness of nature itself. Paul Davies writes, "If the divine underpinning of the laws is removed, their existence becomes a profound mystery. Where do they come from? Who sent the message? Who devised the code?"

How can inanimate objects like molecules and electrons follow laws? Our experience as Humans is that only rational and conscious agents can obey instructions. It remains deeply mysterious how things can do anything whatsoever, let alone abide by Mathematical rules. And what rules! Throughout the history of Science its practitioners have found that anomalies in known laws arc usually accounted for by even deeper and more beautiful laws that seem to underlie the workings of nature.

Many believers and non-believers can find common ground, in their shared reverence for the grandeur of creation. Yet the mind that reflects on nature's intricate order is irresistibly propelled to ask how this order came to be. Doesn't the lawful order of nature require an explanation? If it does, then clearly the best explanation for why the Universe is so orderly and intelligible and favorable for life is that an intelligent being made it that way. <u>There is a Designer–a God</u> who designed the Universe, the World we live in on planet Earth and Man, whom He created in His own image.

Through Science, we now have powerful and convincing evidence that our Human Destiny is part of the Divine Plan and that we live in a meaningful and purposeful world that was made "just so" for us Human Beings by God who created us in His own image. Wow!!

In summary, think of this–of all the Living Beings in the World, only one seeks–Truth, Beauty and Goodness. Only one is thrilled and moved by music. Only one has a sense of awe and wonder at the beauty of Nature–flowers, snow-capped mountains, the oceans, thunder and lightening. Only Humans are created in God's Image. You and me are pretty special; we were made that way.

Chapter #3

The Story of Man

In the Bible, the second account of Creation, states: "God created Man in the likeness of **ourselves** to be the Master of the Earth and all living things. From the dust of the Earth, He fashioned Man and breathed life into him; put him in an innocent state into Paradise." Satan, the great deceiver and liar, tempted Adam and Eve, promising them, "You will not die; you will have knowledge and be like Gods" . . . and then came **the Fall**, the primordial disaster for Man. They broke God's commandment not to eat of the Tree of Knowledge. **By this act, they defied God. They now knew Good and they now knew Evil as well and were thus subject to doing Evil as well as Good**. They were then banished from Paradise for their **rebellion against God. They and all their descendants in the Human Race became subject to sin and death.**

Ever since "The Fall", through all of History, the story is repeated by everyone in every Age—**Man does Good and . . . Man does Evil. We have Free Will and decide to do one thing and not the other**. We decide to follow in obedience to God's Commandments or . . . not to. On the one hand our Conscience tells us what we ought to do (or not do) but on the other hand our Ego moves us to do what we want to do; to satisfy our drives, desires and appetites—for Power, Money, Sex, Revenge and all the other "Worldly Delights".

*   *   *

In the story of Man, down through the ages, men have been subjects, slaves or enemies. Examples are–Greece, Persia, China, Rome. Men were "objects"—things to be ruled, enslaved or killed. It is no different today—people are still enslaved, not by Kings, Emperors, Kahns, or Sultans but the new reigning power—**the Nation-State; Man is still enslaved, brutalized, controlled and killed**. Here is a personal story of a man who paid with his life by refusing to be a slave. In World War II, a Catholic Priest, Father Alfred Delp, wrote this before he was executed by the Nazis:

"Humans need freedom. As slaves, fettered and confined, they are bound to deteriorate. We have spent a great deal of thought and time on external freedom; we have made serious efforts to secure our personal liberty and yet we have lost it again and again. The worst thing is that eventually humans come to accept the state of bondage—it becomes habitual and they hardly notice it. The most abject slaves can be made to believe that the condition in which they are held is actually freedom.

During these long weeks of confinement I have learned by personal experience that a person is truly lost, is the victim of circumstances and oppression only when he is incapable of a great inner sense of depth and freedom. Anyone whose natural element is not an atmosphere of freedom, unassailable and unshakable whatever force may be put on it, is already lost; but such a person is not really a human being any more; he is merely an object, a number, a voting paper. And the inner freedom can only be attained if we have discovered the means of widening our own horizons. We must

progress and grow; we must mount above our own limitations. It can be done; the driving force is the inner urge to conquer whose very existence shows that human nature is fundamentally designed for this expansion. A rebel, after all, can be trained to be a decent citizen, but an idler and a dreamer is a hopeless proposition."

*   *   *

The Judeo-Christian religion started a startling new concept in the story of Man; a new chapter in the Book of Life that Man was created by God with God-given Rights. He was now a Person. Every Man had these Rights—not just Kings, Emperors, Rulers. This religion over thousands of years gave birth to Western Civilization.

We Christians believe the Bible. God tells us, through the ages, that He has not abandoned us. He still lives and acts in His Body—the Catholic Church—which is composed of Sinners (due to our fallen state) trying to become Saints. We fall a lot—but we still get up. We have Hope. We have Faith and we have Love. It's not easy being a good Catholic in this society. Consider how far, as a culture, we have fallen. For a thousand years, Western Civilization developed and promoted: the Family, the idea of limited Government, the Rule of Law, the relief of suffering, the dignity of each individual and on and on.

In our Society today, Secularism reigns supreme—in our courts of Law, in our Governments, in our Universities, Businesses, the Media–Press, TV, Publications. Religion is now banished, marginalized or trivialized. The "powers-that-be" reign supreme now that superstition, discarded traditions and foolish beliefs have been eliminated; so they believe.

There is a constant and powerful effort to eliminate God. Man now is the measure of all things

Christian virtues in society and civilization for over 2,000 years are now marginalized and almost gone. We now have the, "Gimme Generation"–"I'm entitled", the "What's in it for me?" mentality is promoted and often forced upon us from the cradle to the grave. Friedrich Nietzsche famously stated, "God is dead." The death of God has opened Pandora's Box–the Furies have been loosened. Our Society is going down the drain; very ugly and dangerous for all of us.

What do we see as a result? Abortion, Violence, War, Brutality, Sodomy, Child Abuse, Drugs, Sex Obsession, Disease, Suicides, Genocide, Theft, Massive Unhappiness and a TOTAL lack of Meaning to Life. No Beauty, No Truth, No Goodness, No Love of God or neighbor–that's what the, "I've got to be me–I'll decide what's right or wrong" belief has brought about–and that's what most people have bought into.

We are now facing a Post-Human Future. The great political struggles of the twentieth century waged against totalitarianisms of the right and of the left have blinded people to a deeper and darker truth about the present age. East as well as West are traveling in the same utopian direction; all march eagerly to the drums of progress and fly proudly **the banner of Modern Science**. Leading the triumphal procession is modern medicine, which is becoming ever more powerful.

Contemplating present and projected advances in genetic and reproductive technologies, in neuroscience and psychopharmacology, in the development of artificial organs and computer-chip implants for human brains, and in research to retard aging, we now recognize new uses for biotechnical power that soar beyond the traditional medical goals of healing disease and relieving suffering. Human nature itself lies on the operating table, ready for alteration, for eugenic and neuropsychic "enhancement", for wholesale redesign. New creators are confidently amassing their powers and quietly honing their skills, while on the street their evangelists are zealously prophesying a posthuman future. For anyone who cares about preserving our humanity, the time has come to pay attention.

Answers to the question, "**What is Personhood**?", depend not on Science or even on ethics but on proper anthropology; one that richly understands what it means to be a Human Being, in our bodily, psychic, social, cultural, political, and spiritual dimensions. There is a deep connection between perversions of our soul that characterize the entire society. To say "yes" to baby manufacture is to say "no" to all natural human relations. A society, when it does procreate, that sees its children as **projects** rather than as **gifts** is unlikely ever to be open to the question of the meaning and dignity of procreation. What is urgently needed is a richer, more natural biology and anthropology; one that does full justice to the meaning of our peculiarly human union of soul and body. We can learn from thinking about Genesis what it means that the Earth's most godlike creature is made of dirt and life-giving breath.

The Human Being as a Person is a Unique "Species" in the Animal World

You and I as Beings are, "**Human Beings**".

In the Bible, Genesis states that God created Adam and Eve. God is the Creator. We are His Creatures. Special Creatures created in God's

Image–how extraordinary! Our own existence as a Human Being began in our Mother's womb and each of us became a **Person**. Thus begins the first relationship of one person to another person; the "me and you" relationship of a baby to his Mother. **Thus begins a Life and a Personality**. A man's personality is developed during his life by how he acts and is acted upon by his relationships with other persons.

Personhood is inextricably tied up with, "the other," i.e., the other person. For our entire life, we have relationships with other people. We learn to rely on some and avoid others. Those we trust, we rely on; **we have Faith in them**. Experience tells us they can be trusted. Not just those we know who have proven themselves reliable but even those we don't know: when getting into an airplane or an elevator; eating food prepared by someone else; driving at 55mph on one side of the road with another driver going the same speed in the other direction. **Faith is a reality of every person's life, every bit as much as Reason. In short, Faith and Reason together are essential to every person's life. The question, the fundamental question, is Faith in what?** Is our Faith grounded in experience? Is it grounded in Reason? Do we believe our Faith is solidly grounded whether that Faith is in things, people or God? The answer to these questions should determine what you should plan to do with your Life–in this world and the next.

Man is less than the angels, higher than animals. Man is unique–an Embodied Soul. This Soul is the core of human life. It's "Animation"; it's "Vitalism"; it's "Spirit." It is the essence of being alive.

The Human Being is the highest form of life on Earth; a distinctive and unique life form. Fingerprints/DNA show the uniqueness of each individual. Furthermore, each human being that has ever lived is absolutely unique. Isn't this incredible? No two Human Beings (even identical twins) are the same. Talk about being special!! (Out of millions of people alive today, not one has an identical fingerprint to any other person or an identical pattern in the iris of a person's eye. Fantastically unique!)

Each individual Person is shaped by two factors—your Nature and your Nurture.

A person's Nature is exclusive; it is one-of-a-kind. No other person who has ever lived has an identical fingerprint or eye-print as yours—and so it is with your entire body and mind—it is your <u>Nature</u>.

A person's <u>Nurture</u> is formed by all the persons and events he meets and experiences from his birth to his death. Powerful influences of persons in our lives will shape what we think and what we do as well as events one can't control (i.e., war, injury, winning the lotto and such).

Each Human Being has what no other animal has:

- A Conscience—in our core of Being, we know there is a Law of "Right and Wrong"
- Consciousness
- Curiosity, the Urge to Explore
- Love
- A Sense of Wonder at Great Music, Prose, Poetry, the Beauties of Nature
- Laughter—Humor
- Ethics and Morality

The Human Being is unique among Living Beings. He is an "Embodied Soul"; with a Mind, a Body and a Spirit.

As a living animal, I am born, grow, grow old and die. But I am more than an animal; I have a Soul and–I also have a Mind; which has four powers–Intellect, Memory, Imagination and Will.

As a person, I am always becoming someone other than I was–but I know no matter how different I am, I'm still the same person; "Me" is still "Me" no matter how much I've changed–physically, mentally, emotionally and spiritually.

Man has a Soul, a Spirit. The proof of a Spirit's reality is evident at death–the life force, the vitality and animation are gone.

When God created Man and gave him a Soul in the "Image of God," he gave Man a vast potential–to live forever after Mortal Death. He is destined for Eternity.

The new biotechnologies threaten liberty and equality—"human dignity." For man is the only being on earth that can experience wonder and awe at the rich and incredible facts of life, the soul and human awareness. Appreciative wonder and respectful awe before the mystery of life is indispensible if we are to be able to defend life's dignity against the deadly distortions of scientific abstraction.

Transforming powers are already here. The Pill. *In vitro* fertilization. Bottled embryos. Surrogate wombs. Cloning. Genetic screening. Genetic manipulation. Organ harvesting. Mechanical spare parts. Chimeras. Brain implants. Ritalin for the young, Viagra for the old, Prozac for everyone.

Aldous Huxley's Brave New World, 1932: Huxley's portrays a dystopia that goes *with*, rather than against, the human grain. Indeed, it is animated by our most humane and progressive aspirations. Following those aspirations to their ultimate realization, Huxley enables us to recognize those less obvious but often more pernicious evils that are inextricably linked to the successful attainment of partial goods.

Huxley depicts human life seven centuries hence, living under the gentle hand of humanitarianism rendered fully competent by genetic manipulation, psychoactive drugs, hypnopaedia and high-tech amusements. At long last, mankind has succeeded in eliminating disease, aggression, war, anxiety, suffering, guilt, envy and grief. But this victory comes at the heavy price of homogenization, mediocrity, trivial pursuits, shallow attachments, debased tastes, spurious contentment and souls without loves or longings. The Brave New World has achieved prosperity, community, stability and near-universal contentment, only to be inhabited by creatures of human shape but stunted humanity. They consume, fornicate, take "soma," enjoy "centrifugal bumble-puppy," and operate the machinery that makes it all possible. They do not read, write, think, love, or govern themselves. Art and Science, virtue and religion, family and friendship are passé. What matters most is bodily health and immediate gratification: "Never put off till tomorrow the fun you can have today." No one aspires to anything higher. Brave New Man is so dehumanized that he does not even realize what has been lost.

The society of the future will deliver exactly what we want most—health, safety, comfort, plenty, pleasure, peace of mind and length of days—we can reach the same humanly debased condition solely by free human choice. No need for World Controllers. Just give us the technological imperative, liberal democratic society, compassionate humanitarianism, moral pluralism and free markets, and we can take ourselves to a Brave New World all by ourselves–without even deliberately deciding to go. In case you haven't noticed, the train has already left the station and is gathering speed, although there appears to be no human hands on the throttle.

There are some who are delighted by this state of affairs: some scientists and biotechnologists, their entrepreneurial backers and a cheering claque of sci-fi enthusiasts, futurologists and libertarians. There are dreams to be realized, powers to be exercised, honors to be won and money–big money–to be made. Many of us are worried; we can see all too clearly where the train is headed, and we do not like the destination. We can distinguish cleverness about means from wisdom about ends, and we are loath to entrust the future of the race to those who cannot tell the difference. No friend of humanity cheers for a posthuman future.

Finally, and perhaps most troubling, our views of the meaning of our humanity have been so transformed by the scientific-technological approach to the world and to life that we are in danger of forgetting what we have to lose; and it is a huge and devastating loss–our Humanity.

How will the Story of Man end? Only God, the Author of the Story, knows. If the Secular Humanists are right–Believers and non-Believers become extinct—dead, dead, dead . . . they think. But . . . if Christians are right by saying, "Yes" to God, Eternal Life is theirs and Heaven awaits. To those who say "No" to God, Satan claims those Souls in Hell for all Eternity.

So this is the exciting challenge facing each of you—to be the "good yeast" in Society to bring about renewal. The story will end for me when I die and stand before God and the Book of my Life is judged–gulp! I'd better get busy.

* * *

So far, we've reviewed the Story of the Race of Man down through the Ages. This is important to know. Closer to home is the realization that each one of us Human Beings have our own personal story to tell–the Story of My Life. Stories are how we tell what happens to us; how we live and move and have our Being; how we act and interact with others during our life.

There was a famous book written some 70 years ago entitled, "*The Greatest Story Ever Told.*" It was a story of the birth, life and death of Jesus Christ. This truly is the Greatest Story as it involves all of Humanity and each of us in the Drama of Life with God as the Author. There are innumerable other stories; some are tragic, inane, vile or worthless; others are heroic, noble, decent, full of goodness, beauty and truth.

The most important story in your life is Your Story. You are the main character in the drama and also the playwright. Likewise for me. I hope to tell my story, and I hope you tell yours, by our actions, day by day, as if our lives depend on it as it surely does, both in this World and the next. The questions to be asked to frame "The Story of You" are these—

- Who am I? What am I?
- Where am I going? What am I doing with my life?
- How do I get there from here?
- What is the meaning of life?

Remember what Pope John Paul II said, "**Be Not Afraid**"!! Be a proud and staunch witness to your Beliefs. Do this and you can join all Christians in "Solidarity" to bring the "Springtime" of Christianity in the 21st Century.

Chapter #4

Faith and Reason

Man needs Faith and Reason.

One without the other is like a runner with one leg expecting to compete for a Gold medal in the Olympics . . . it's just not going to happen.

Faith is in no way opposed to Reason. Rather, Faith is the only way to discover truths that are beyond the domain of reason.

For Atheists, Faith evokes images of Santa Claus and the Easter Bunny; beliefs appropriate for children but certainly not for adults. Science "asks us to take nothing on Faith." Faith seems to qualify as a kind of mental illness for Secular Humanists.

At first glance the Athesist hostility to Faith seems puzzling. All of us make decisions based on Faith all the time. We routinely trust in authorities and take actions based on statements and actions that we don't or can't verify. We were not present at the Battle of Britain, but are quite sure it happened. We may have never been to Australia, but are sure that it is there because we trust the word of others who have been there. We trust maps of the World. We have Faith in air traffic controllers and the skill of pilots every time we board an airplane.

So thoroughly do we rely on Faith that modern life would become impossible were we to insist on evidence and verification before acting on doing anything. How do we know the cereal is safe to eat? How can we be sure our car is not going to blow up when we turn on the ignition? Why should we take it for granted that the person whose voice I hear at the other end of the telephone is really there? How do we know our vote for a presidential candidate will be counted?

For the believer, Faith delivers the goods. Faith in God is routinely vindicated in everyday life. People come to trust God for His fidelity and love in the same way they come to trust their spouses.

Religious Faith is not merely about what satisfies Human wants and needs, but also about what is true. Faith makes claims of a special kind. The soul is immortal and lives after death. There is a God in Heaven who seeks us. Heaven awaits those who trust in God; those who reject Him are headed for the other place.

Through Revelations, we have Faith in a person–Jesus Christ. If there is a Divine Being who created the Universe with special concern for us as Human Beings, then it is entirely reasonable to suppose that, absent our ability to find Him, He will find His way to us. Faith is a gift; it is God's way of disclosing Himself to us through Divine Revelation.

Religious Faith is not in opposition to reason. The purpose of Faith is to discover truths that are of the highest importance to us yet are unavailable to us through purely natural means. A wise man once said, "Even if all possible scientific questions are answered, the problems of life have still not been answered at all."

The most important questions of life are: Why am I here? What should I love? What should I live for?

The believer uses Faith to gain access to a new domain, that of Revelation. The believer embraces Faith not "blindly". He expects Revelation to reactivate and guide his reason. Social critic Michael Novak says that, "using reason is a little like using the naked eye, whereas 'putting on Faith' is like putting on perfectly calibrated glasses . . . to capture otherwise invisible dimensions of reality."

The Christian also has Faith to trust in things he cannot prove by physical evidence; his Faith is based on Trust–Trust in Eyewitnesses–thousands of people who saw Christ and witnessed His Miracles; the testimony of the Apostles, His Mother and St. Paul that He rose from the dead and ascended before their very eyes and . . . the thousands of Martyrs who gave their lives rather than deny Jesus Christ. Jesus Christ, our Savior, who rose from the dead on Easter morning for the salvation of all Mankind.

The Believer uses Faith <u>and Reason</u> to answer the most important questions of Life–Why am I here? Who should I love? Does my Life have any meaning? What should I think? What should I do? What happens when I die? These questions cannot be answered by the use of Reason alone. Neither by Science, as these are questions beyond Reason, beyond Physics–they are Mysteries.

The Unbeliever uses his Reason, but scorns Faith in things not material and is at the mercy of the World, the Flesh and the Devil.

Secular Humanists define a Person as <u>Material</u> . . . period. He is just an <u>Object</u> like every other thing on Earth; in short–<u>he is a Thing</u>.

A Christian defines a Person as a Being with a Soul as well as a body. He is a unique Being; he is the <u>subject</u> of thought, not the object. As a person, he has God-given rights–Life, Dignity, Free-Will.

Emmanuel Kant (acknowledged as one of the smartest Philosophers that ever lived) stated: "Reason's final step is to recognize that there are an infinite number of things that surpass it."

Faith is in no way opposed to Reason. Rather, Faith is the only way to discover truths that are beyond the domain of reason and experience. Philosopher and Mathematician Blaise Pascal argued that the Athesist's wager against God's existence is manifestly unreasonable. Given what we know and don't know about what is to come after death, there is no alternative but to weigh the odds. We discover that from the perspective of Reason itself, Faith is the smart bet. It makes sense to have Faith.

Blaise Pascal begins his argument against the Atheists with this statement, "Reason's final step is to recognize that there are an infinite number of things which surpass it."

The ingenuity of Pascal's argument for an after-life is that it emphasizes the practical necessity of making a choice. This necessity is imposed by death. The unavoidability of the decision exposes the sheer stupidity of "<u>apatheism</u>." The refusal to choose becomes a choice–a choice against God. This is a matter of life and death.

Pascal thus exposes the Nobel pose of the Atheist who fancies himself as a brave and lonely man facing the abyss. But what would we think of a man who stands ready to face a horrible fate that he has a chance to avert?

Agnostics say: "I cannot believe because I simply don't know." This attitude is peculiar for two reasons. First, it is entirely incurious about the most important questions of life: Why are we here? Is this life all there is? What happens when we die? Their attitude is also bizarre because it shows no hint of an awareness of the limits of reason. Empirical evidence is unavailable because the senses cannot penetrate a realm beyond experience. Faith is a statement of trust in what we do not know for sure. Faith says that even though I don't know something with certainty, I believe it to be true because I trust God's Word; His Revelation. I trust the thousands of people who saw and heard Jesus Christ. I trust the word of the Apostles and Disciples who saw Christ after His Resurrection from the dead.

Atheism teaches that Human Beings are nothing but flesh and bone, brains, arteries, blood and organs; Man is a kind of intelligent robot, a carbon-based computer.

Atheist Scientists don't believe in the Soul and believe it is absurd to believe a non-physical entity can move or influence a material object like the brain. They believe we live in a deterministic Universe and that Free Will doesn't exist; it is an illusion.

Secular Humanist Richard Dawkins argues that although we are the product of our selfish genes, "we have the power to turn against our Creators. We, alone on earth, can rebel against the tyranny of the selfish replicators. If we, "understand what our own selfish genes are up to . . . we have the chance to upset their design." If this is true, then by Dawkin's own admission, we Humans occupy a unique position because our minds can control our material body. For Dawkins to say that we can declare ourselves independent of our selfish genes makes no sense. The key word here is "chosen," which presumes free choice. Dawkins has not explained where this free choice has come from. How has the human inclination to avoid having children survived the process of natural selection? "Genes say reproduce, but I say go to hell." Moreover, how can happiness and virtue be something "for us to determine"? Where and "who" is this "us"? How do we get the ingenuity and strength to battle a foe as formidable as our own nature?

Francis Crick is a brilliant Scientist who is an Atheist. In Crick's view, the brain "sees," "hears," "believes," "guesses," and even makes "interpretations." But as Philosopher Peter Hacker and Neuroscientist Max Bennett point out, it is a conceptual fallacy to attribute qualities to the brain that are possessed only by persons. My brain isn't conscious; I am conscious. My brain isn't thinking; I am thinking. Crick is guilty of something called the pathetic fallacy, which is the fallacy of ascribing human qualities to inanimate objects. Certainly we use our brains to perceive and reason, just as we use our hands and feet to play tennis. But it is just as crazy to say my hands and feet are playing tennis as it is to say my racket is playing tennis. By the same token it is wrong to portray the brain as perceiving, feeling, thinking, or even being aware of anything; it is my mind that is conscious and makes decisions.

Chapter #5

The Conscience of Man and Free Will

There is a deeper problem with extending the materialistic understanding of Nature to Human Beings. For starters, we experience the outside World—the World described by the laws of Physics and Chemistry—very differently than we experience ourselves. All other things we experience indirectly, from the outside, through the apparatus of our senses, but ourselves we experience directly, from the inside, without the involvement of our senses. Only about ourselves do we have this kind of "inside information," which is the clearest, most fundamental knowledge we can have. We know that the external account of reality, however accurate it may be in describing raindrops and cheetahs, is not the full story when it comes to describing ourselves.

We are sure, for example, that we exist. David Hume, a famous Philosopher Atheist, said that we can't really even know this: "When I enter most intimately into what I call *myself*, I always stumble on some particular perception or other, or heat or cold, light or shade, love or hate, pain or pleasure. I never can catch *myself* at any time without a perception and never can observe any thing but the perception." Consequently, for Hume, the self is a fiction because it cannot be empirically located. But the remarkable thing is that we are conscious of our own existence prior to having any feelings and thoughts. Besides, our feelings and thoughts are experienced as "possessions" somehow distinct from the self, as the self is experienced directly. Schopenhauer, a famous Philosopher, writes that as we are the subjects of our own inquiry, the materialist mistake is that of "the subject that forgets to take account of itself"!

We not only exist, but we are also conscious. This consciousness is totally basic: we cannot get "behind" it. Moreover, human consciousness seems to be of a different order than animal consciousness. Human behavior makes the most sense when it is explained in terms of beliefs and desires, not in terms of volts and grams.

There is no Scientific explanation of how atoms and molecules can produce something as radical, original and non-physical as Consciousness. The materialist understanding of human experience seems inadequate because we experience our lives as a unity. The matter that makes up my body changes constantly, and yet I remain the same person. Our self-conception is strongly rooted in memory of past experiences, without which it is not clear that the "self" would retain any meaning at all.

Secular Humanists state as Fact (not Theory) that our mental processes are determined totally and wholly by the physical motion of atoms in the brain. Christian Philosophers with a rapier thrust respond—"If that is so, I have no reason to suppose my beliefs are true . . . and hence I have no reason for supposing my brain is composed of atoms."

Our ideas about Scientific theories . . . assume we are rational beings who are free to observe the Universe as we want and to draw logical deductions from what we see.

Astro-physicist, Stephen Hawking (an Atheist) states: "The only answer I can give to this problem is based on Darwin's principle of natural selection." Hawking's solution is based on a non sequitur. Biologists invoke evolution to explain the challenges primitive man faced in prehistoric environments. But evolution cannot explain more than this. There are no survival instincts or pressures that require man to develop the capacity to understand the rotation of the planets or the microscopic content of matter. Moreover, evolution selects only for reproduction and survival, not for truth.

Dinesh D'Souza in his book, *"What's so Great about Christianity,"* states the strongest argument against materialism. It is the argument for Free Will. He states: "Let me illustrate. I am sitting at my computer with a cup of coffee on my desk. I can reach over and take a sip if I choose; I can just leave the cup alone and let the coffee get cold. Now I ask: is there anything in the laws of physics that forces me to do any of these things? Obviously not. In Milton Friedman's phrase, I am "free to choose." This freedom characterizes many, although not all, of the actions in my life. I am not free to stop breathing while I am asleep, nor am I free to control the passage of food through my intestines. I am, however, free to knock my coffee mug on the floor. Now once I decide to do this, my choice is determined by no scientific law but rather by my free decision.

Immanuel Kant deepens this argument into the domain of Morality. He reasons that, "We are moral beings. We have moral concepts like "right" and "wrong" and "good" and "evil." We "ought" to do this and "ought not" to do that. Try as we can, we cannot avoid this way of thinking and acting. Morality is an empirical fact no less real than any other experience in the world." Kant argues that for these concepts to have any meaning, it must be the case that we have a choice. *Ought* implies *can*. If determinism is true, then no one in the world can ever refrain from anything that he or she does. The whole of morality—not just this morality or that morality but morality itself—becomes an illusion. Our whole vocabulary of praise and blame, admiration and contempt, approval and disapproval would have to be eradicated. People who operate outside the sphere of morality we call psychopaths. We are, by our nature, moral. And it follows from this that we are free to choose between alternative courses of action.

Kant follows this train of reasoning to its remarkable conclusion: we enjoy a measure of freedom in the operation of our will. This freedom means doing what we want to do or what we ought to do, as opposed to what we have to do. Part of what we think and do is not governed by a necessity imposed by the laws of Science.

Thus it is clear that there is a part of our Humanity that is subject to the world of Science, but also, and this is much more important, there is a part of our Humanity that is outside the realm of Scientific laws. We live in the realm of the Phenomenal, which is the material realm. But we also live in the realm of the Noumenal, which is the realm of freedom. It is the Noumenal realm, the realm outside Space and Time, that makes possible free choices, which are implemented within the realm of Space and Time. Materialism makes us Humans live in two dimensions—Space and Time, whereas in reality we Humans exist in three dimensions—Space, Time and also the Meta-Physical—Meta-Physical concerns a Reality above and beyond all physical things.

To some, it may seem fantastic that all of Nature should obey fixed laws, but that a single type of animal—hairy, omnivorous, and bipedal—should be able to act above these laws. Yet, we are that animal. The material world is not the only world there is; for there is a higher domain we rely on in every free choice we make.

The Human Being is unique among living beings. He is an animal of the genre—"Homo"—in the animal kingdom but he is more than that—he is an "Embodied Soul." When God created Man and gave him a Soul in the "Image of God", He gave Man a vast potential—he is destined for Eternity, to live forever after his mortal life on earth.

Let us follow the wise counsel of Pope John Paul II—"Be not afraid." Show your Christianity in the way you live by loving God and our fellow Man. If we act in "solidarity" with each other, we will experience a "Springtime"—a flowering in the World of Truth, Beauty and Goodness.

Chapter #6

Mystery

What do Secular Humanists say about Mysteries? Either–"nothing" or "they don't exist." They are in total denial. And, yet, Mysteries abound: in the Universe/in our World/at the Atomic level/inside our bodies, inside our brains, inside our Souls. The Ultimate Mysteries are Spiritual.

Miracles can be viewed as suspensions of the laws of Nature; there is nothing in Science or logic that says this cannot happen. For God there are clearly no constraints on His infinite power. Modern Physics concedes that beyond the natural world the laws of nature do not apply. This is the point of Miracles, to disrupt the normal course of things to draw attention to something happening which is amazing to those who see it happening. God made the Universe; He also made the Laws of Nature, and He alters them when He chooses.

Arthur Schopenhauer was a famous Philosopher and Atheist. This is his comment on the mysterious world of Magic~

"To smile in advance at all magic, we have to find the world completely intelligible. But this we can only do when we look into it with an extremely shallow gaze that admits of no inkling that we are plunged into a sea of riddles and incomprehensibilities and have no

thorough and direct knowledge and understanding either of things or ourselves."

As with Magic—so it is, and it is even more inexplicable, with Mystery. Here are examples of Mystery in the Universe and the World:

1. Before the <u>Big Bang</u> . . . there was nothing. What is nothing?

2. The <u>Universe</u> is expanding; expanding into what?

3. What is <u>Infinity</u>?

4. Who made the Universe? Life could not exist on Earth; we Humans wouldn't even be here "but for" the <u>Six Immense Forces</u> that came into being at the instant of the "Big Bang."

5. Who made the <u>Laws of Science</u>? Every Law we know–every one has had a Law Giver who made that Law–Kings, Emperors, Khans, Nation States. What about the absolute Laws of Science? Certainly not Scientists; they only <u>discover</u> what the Laws of Science are. Who do you think made the Laws of Science which govern the whole Universe.

6. What is <u>Energy</u>? We know the <u>forms</u> of Energy but what gives it such power? Where does it come from?

7. What causes <u>Gravity</u>? Isaac Newton sees an apple fall to earth and says, "Ah-ha!" And, then proves his famous Theory of Gravity in the physical world. But the Mystery is this: What is

the Force that causes this to happen? Where did it come from? What keeps it going? All these are mysterious.

8. <u>Micro-Mysteries:</u> Scientists draw a picture to show the relationship of electrons/protons and neutrons to each other and how they interact but <u>no Scientist knows what the actual structure of an Atom is</u>.

9. <u>Quantum Mechanics</u>—on bombarding Atoms—a Mystery results—is the Atom a wave or a particle? It acts like both; to <u>Scientists</u> this is puzzling; it is a Mystery.

10. Splitting the Hydrogen Atom—causing it to split apart results in an enormous Force resulting in the "H" bomb. What is this Force? Where does it come from?

11. How does <u>Life</u> start? How do Scientists explain our Consciousness, or our Conscience? How do Scientists explain the Act of Mind, which is mental (not physical!) to do or not do something? They don't and they can't–it's not physical.

12. <u>Microbiology</u>—physically, we ourselves are profoundly mysterious. How do we come to life as Human Beings? What causes our animation—our Life Force? What Scientist can explain how all the cells "know" when and how to specialize and become eyes, legs, brains, or how cells replicate; work together as "Command Centers"; or give specific instructions to muscles, nerves, and various sympathetic systems which function independently without us thinking or acting?

The issue of Miracles is of special importance to Christians, because Christianity is the only major religion in the World that depends on Miracles. Christianity relies on them. Paul writes in his first letter to the Corinthians 15:14 that without Christ's Resurrection, "our preaching is useless and so is your faith." Christ's Resurrection is far from the only Miracle reported in the New Testament. Christ performed Miracles all the time. He walked on water, quieted the storm, fed the multitudes, healed the blind, and brought Lazarus back from the dead. Only if Miracles are possible is Christianity believable.

Chapter #7

I—Science

The Foundation of Science began with primitive Man—learning "**how to**"—start a fire, make a wheel, shape weapons, build wells, domesticate the horse, make tools, and on and on. Early Civilizations in Mesopotamia, Egypt, the Americas, China and India all developed their own separate cultures, languages, mathematics, writings by men of intellect, learning "**how to**" do more and more complicated things. This was "Knowledge".

The Romans, 3000 years ago, built bridges, pontoons, aqueducts, arches, huge temples, an intricate road system (the "Via Apia") and a system of combat (the Roman Square) which made them invincible. They called what their engineers and mathematicians did—"Scientia"—this translates in English to the word—"Knowledge". From this word—"Scientia"—the word "Science" came into being and has applied to ideas, inventions and technology ever since.

Knowledge is the root of Science. Of all that has been learned over thousands of years. The goal of Science is to know about every thing in the Universe.

Science, <u>pure Science</u>, in all its various fields is doing amazing things to better Mankind. Science, however, has been used to also make things which do enormous harm. <u>Scientists can work for the good of Mankind, or do "Science" which harms Mankind</u>. (Hitler's Scientists and Stalin's Scientists come to mind.)

Science has excellent methods and technology to expand Man's knowledge about how things do what they do and using that knowledge allows Scientists to invent things which help Humanity in so many good ways. Unfortunately, there is another side to the coin; those things can also be used to do great harm to Humanity—examples are the atomic bomb, germ warfare and genetic manipulation. Science is not the answer to Man's existence. It is using reason to solve problems and improve Man's existence on Earth. This is all it can and should do.

A Scientist doesn't <u>Invent</u> the—
   1. Laws of Physics (of inanimate things).
   2. The Laws of Biology (the laws of all living entities).

What he does do is discover that these Laws exist—that they are real and absolute. Also, he learns that other non-physical realities also exist—Mathematics, music, thinking, emotions are real, very real. Abstract laws exist whether "man" is aware of them or not. (Gravity existed before Scientists discovered it.)

Biologists/Physicists are not creators—they are observers; they learn; they invent and put things together. They make "things". Biologists are now manipulating life forms. Gene splicing—how different in concept is it from the man who put the first wheelbarrow together? How different is it from Luther Burbank who first took a plum tree, spliced a graft of an apricot tree on to it and made a plumcot tree? Gene splicing is enormously more complicated but it is simply high, very high, technology. Nothing is being "created." By manipulating basic life elements—genes and cells—man and his technological wizardry are able to alter, to change, to interrupt the natural and make something different, something un-natural. Scientists in laboratories are now splicing human genes into animals! Monstrous, literally. Talk about Dr. Frankenstein! They are referred to "Scientifically" as "Chimeras." The word comes from a monstrous creature of Greek Mythology—part lion, part serpent and part goat. Something enormously horrid is happening—man is playing at God. Maybe next a Superman, a mental genius, an immortal! And, thereafter, a race of Supermen to run the world. Nietzsche and Hitler would be so proud of the craftsmanship of their heirs.

The more Science expands Man's frontiers of knowledge of the macro/micro worlds, the more complicated and mysterious it all becomes. Time warps/quasars/black holes/ white stars. The sub-atomic level—"left/right handedness". Positrons/ neutrinos. The wave/quantum paradox. **There are immutable and absolute physical laws—the speed of light (maybe), gravity, birth and death—these are Ultimate Realities. These realities exist regardless of what anyone thinks.** Music and Math have structure and laws but they are not material things either; they are Abstract (non-physical) Realities; they are real; very real. They exist independent of what anyone thinks or believes.

II–Science and Mystery

With amazing technological tools and techniques Scientists have probed the physical Universe. They have now proven what the boundaries of their specialized knowledge are. They can probe no further in Micro-Physics and Micro-Biology but only speculate and theorize about—Black Holes, Quarks, Anti-Matter and such. In other words, Scientists have gone as far as they can go; they are confronting Mystery.

As other Scientists probe the <u>Macro-Universe</u>, they also run into astonishing information—the Universe was created . . . out of <u>Nothing</u>! Not only was the Universe created but the Universe is expanding! Scientists have shown this conclusively through precise measurement of electromagnetic radiation called the "Red Shift." This put "paid" to a Theory of cyclical world formations devised to discount the "Big Bang" Theory of a one-time event. As a result, Astrophysicists now have proven an expanding Universe. Expanding into what? Infinity. And, what exactly is Infinity? No one knows. In other words, it is a Mystery.

<u>Infinity defies any logical explanation but there it is—a Mystery we can see before our very eyes by looking up! Mystery abounds in Science today—from Astrophysics to Microbiology</u>—matter is energy (in a solid form). What is energy anyhow? No one really knows. The form of energy which we are most familiar with is—electrical—here again, however, we only know how it works, in certain situations, but not why the structures/relationships are

what they are and where the activity ("vitalism"), what we call energy, <u>comes from or how it originated.</u>

These are Mysteries. Mystery not only surrounds us. We ourselves are imbedded in Mystery as "Embodied Souls." What happens to us when we die? This is the **<u>ULTIMATE MYSTERY</u>**!!!

III—Science and Religion

Science and Religion are both searching for Truth. Science searches for Truth in the Natural World. Religion searches for Truth in the Super-natural World.

In the Bible, Genesis states that Man was made in the "image" and "likeness" of God. This means that there is a spark of divine reason in Man, setting him apart from all other living beings. The ability to reason in Humans was given to Man by the Divine Intelligence that created the Universe.

Let's look at the facts; the uncontroverted Historical Evidence to see if these Secular Humanist Atheists are trying to mislead us with falsehoods.

Secular Humanists state as fact—their Scientific Dogma that Science was founded in the 17th century in revolt against Religious Dogma. **This is a brazen lie!!** Let's look at 1000 years of History to see how Science developed and see what the Evidence is. **In other words, let's look for the Truth**. Secular Humanists state that Religion is the enemy of Science and has been from the beginning. A favorite <u>proof</u>

is Galileo and the Pope—Men of Science vs. Men of Religion. They couldn't be more wrong. Pope Julian was being advised by Scientific Advisors–the leading Astronomers of his time (16th Century). They were the "Scientific Experts;" the then "Establishment". The Scientific Establishment was wrong; Galileo was right. **This is absolute proof that Science is changing all the time in its search for Truth.** The "Establishment" says over and over and over again, as a Mantra, that Faith and Religion are opposed to Science; that they are in conflict. How can that be? Faith is not the same as Religion. What Science and Religion do have in common is–Thinking Man. Man (as a plural noun) and man (as a personal noun) do good things . . . and do evil things.

Religious persons believe and support Science. They always have. Consider this fact, this Truth: **the Catholic Church was the sole founder and developer of Science–all of Science in Western Civilization for over 1000 years!!**

In the twelfth century, the first Universities were founded in Bologna and Paris. Oxford and Cambridge were founded in the early thirteenth century, followed by Universities in Rome, Naples, Salamanca, Seville, Prague, Vienna, Cologne, and Heidelberg. **The Catholic Church founded all of these first Universities** by encouraging and supporting men of Science to expand and explore all knowledge of the World.

The first hospitals and medical research centers were built by Catholics. The first Observatories for Astronomy were built by Catholics and later ones by Christians. **This evidence is overwhelming proof that Religion and Science are not in conflict.**

All peoples of whatever Religion believe God is Truth, immutable Truth, absolute. Whereas, the "Truths" of Science have been, are and continue to be, changing. The "Truths" are the gropings of questioning minds seeking the various levels of truths in things of this earth. Scientists aren't inventing at the micro and macro levels of Physics-the truth is they are finding astounding beauty and intricacies in Nature-they are staring Mystery right in the face. The Catholic Church founded all of the first Universities and thus sought to expand and explore all knowledge of the World.

Bacon, a Catholic, was the founder of the Scientific Method, the "inventor of invention". **This new Scientific Method launched an explosion of innovations and inventions starting in the 13ᵗʰ century. The 14ᵗʰ century was, "one of the great inventive eras of Mankind".** Europe developed a new way of understanding nature and making it work to human purposes.

Here is a list of the Giants of Science in the 13ᵗʰ, 14ᵗʰ, and 15ᵗʰ centuries. They were all Catholics: Copernicus, Kepler, Galileo, Brahe, Descartes, Boyle, Newton, Leibniz, Gassendi. In the later centuries: Pascal, Mersenne, Cuvier, Harvey, Dalton, Faraday, Herschel, Joule, Lyell, Lavoisier, Priestley, Kelvin, Ohm, Ampere, Steno, Pasteur, Maxwell and Planck. The Christian Beliefs of these towering figures of Science were their guiding inspiration and they were the "cutting edge" Scientists of their day.

These are the facts; this is the evidence from the Middle Ages till today; that it was Christianity that formed the cradle of learning, knowledge and

Science in Western Civilization; that all men of Science for thousands of years were Christians; that it wasn't until the 17th Century that the mischief started. What mischief might that be? How about Pride and Arrogance (with new technological trappings)–"Who needs God? MAN is the measure of all things."

Chapter #8

The Two Standards

In the 16th Century Ignatius Loyola, founder of the Society of Jesus (Jesuits), wrote his "Spiritual Exercises" which have been spiritual bedrock of Catholic teaching for hundreds of years, worldwide.

In the Spiritual Exercises, there is a Meditation called, "The Two Standards"—which concerns every Human Being who ever lived (or will live) since God created Adam and Eve. It is an allegorical story of Spiritual Warfare. Here it is . . .

This is a global War waged by two Armies.
The Army on the right has on its Standard a White Flag, emblazoned in gold, with the words God, Angels and Saints.
The Army on the left has as its Standard a Black Flag, on which is emblazoned a Red Dragon breathing flames whose tail is sweeping stars away.
These Armies are engaged in a battle to the death between forces of God and the forces of Satan.
There is an enormous clash as the Armies meet in mortal combat.
The battle is furious; it is a fight to the death. All of Humanity is engaged in the fight; there are no non-combatants; it is all-out War, a War to the death. But it is an unusual War in that the

battle is for the Soul of each Human Being. Victory or defeat is measured by each Army every time a person dies. If the Dragon wins, Satan claims his prize and takes that Soul to Hell. If the White Army wins, God takes that Soul to Heaven. This War has been going on for a long time—and will continue for all time.

This Allegory is more than just an Allegory; it applies in reality to each one of us. You, me and all our fellow Human Beings.

Satan's Army—Secular Humanists

Secular Humanists are Atheists. These Atheists are waging "all out war" against Christians. We will only be able to defend ourselves when we know what our enemy believes; and learn their strengths and weaknesses. So, let's look at what they have said and done to get a clearer picture of the mischief they are up to.

Atheists call themselves, "Religious Humanists." Their "Credo," their basic beliefs, is set forth in two documents: *Humanist Manifesto I* (1933) and *Humanist Manifesto II* (1973). In 1933, Sir Julian Huxley identified and described, "**The Coming New Religion of Humanism**." It is an accurate description of a religion that holds that Man is the measure of all things. It states that—"There is no God." Their Faith, their Belief, is called Scientific Humanism.

It is a Belief that "in the beginning" there was nothing and then nothing happened to the nothing until the nothing magically exploded for no reason creating everything. Then, out of nowhere, a bunch of everything magically arranged

itself for no reason whatsoever into self-replicating bits which then turned themselves into humans who in time could see the vastness and beauty of all Creation.

What kind of a Religion is this? Where is Beauty, Delight and Love in this dreary Religion? Ugh!

Aren't Secular Humanists amazing? <u>They say there is no such thing as Sin</u>; they say Priests invented Sin to make people feel guilty. <u>No more Anger, no more Envy, no more Pride, no more Greed, no more Lust, no more Lying, no more Cheating, no more Hatred. Really? Don't they ever read newspapers or watch TV?</u>

The Scientist who is a Secular Humanist believes the physical world is all there is when it is as plain as the nose on his face that the abstract world is boundless, real . . . and mysterious. <u>Science is not the answer to Man's existence.</u>

Secular Humanists deny that morality depends upon religion. Lenin (a Russian Communist and Disciple of Karl Marx who wrote the *Communist Manifesto*) said, "Every idea of God is unutterable vileness." History, however, shows what happens to a Culture when Religion is destroyed.

Secular Humanists don't believe Man is made in God's image; they believe Man is "nothing but" a thinking animal; "nothing but"—a thinking form of ape. History shows us where this leads—Nietzsche, Karl Marx, Lenin, Hitler, Pol Pot, Mao Tse-tung, Communism, Fascism, Reductionism, Materialism—**<u>Secular Humanism like all other "isms" before it is a Totalitarian Dictatorship.</u>**

Secular Humanists threaten Society and Civilization because they deny the sacredness of Life and the Dignity of each person and each person's unalienable Right to Life. **The "Establishment" —Secular Humanist Scientists walk the corridors of power and rule the Scientific Establishment. No Scientist dares to openly challenge their "Credo"—that there is no God**. All the Honorific awards; top professional chairs, University positions; the publishing of papers in Scientific Journals, are barred to any Scientist who doesn't toe the Party line that there is no God. **Their only God is "Science" itself and guess who the High Priests of Scientism are? Answer: Themselves—the Establishment. Secular Humanism is a Scientific Cult that believes there is no God. A Cult by definition is a group of individuals united in a belief system claimed to be exclusive and true. It is rigid Fundamentalism in that it will tolerate no deviation from its beliefs.** These Scientific Cultists are superior intellectual persons (self-proclaimed) who believe that anyone who doesn't believe as they do is and "Infidel"—"Fanatic," or Ignoramus.

Leading Scientists in Astrophysics, Biology, Anthropology and other sub-sets sail under a "Jolly Roger" at odds with Truth, Beauty and Goodness when they promulgate their beliefs, their "Credo." **They arrogantly state as fact that all other Belief Systems based on Mystery, Morality, Ethics, God, Jesus Christ, Buddhism, Islam are wrong**. They cannot answer Ethical, Moral or Philosophical questions much less questions about God or Eternity. Ethics, law, philosophy, religion, politics and freedom of scientific inquiry are not and cannot be "Scientific"—(by definition).

These Scientists claim exclusivity on Moral, Ethical, Philosophical and Theological questions—(Richard Dawkins, a High-Priest of Secular Humanists claims, as a fact, that he is right because he's smart and everyone else is stupid—this is the height of Arrogance and Pride). Dawkins doesn't just say, "This is what I believe," rather, he pontificates that he, as a Scientist, knows there can't be a God and, therefore, it is an absolute fact there is no God. This is called, "Scientism"—a set of core beliefs which has no Scientific basis.

Scientist Richard Dawkins is a High Priest of Secular Humanism. He sells his personal beliefs as "Facts," as, "Truth," but in this, he fails. No amount of scorn or pejorative language can cure the lack of logic in his core beliefs by "boot strap"/ad hominum or "Strawman" arguments. His hatred of Religion is intense; hatred is an acid that blinds a person.

There is no question that Dawkins is a passionate believer (anyone who has read one of his books knows this). As a High Priest of Secular Atheism, he is as political as any T.V. preacher in marketing his beliefs to the gullible or poorly informed that man is "nothing but"—an animal. (This is a slur on the animal world as animals don't act evil, mean or cruel).

Dawkins is no different than generations of Scientists before him. 2000 years ago there were Greek philosophers who didn't believe in God and argued with Socrates and Plato. Modern believers such as Skinner, Pavlov, Brownowski, still beat the same drum. "There is no God—there is only an intelligent animal—an Ape."

Secular Humanists state as proof that there is no God, only Man —"Darwinism" which is a **Theory** of Evolution. They state as Fact that, "Man exists and, therefore, the fact that Man exists proves it is true." This is a Tautology and is no proof at all. A Theory is not proof of what it claims.

Secular Humanists play what they believe is their "Trump Card" to prove Man is just an animal. That so-called "Trump Card" is—Evolution–they state as Fact that over time, a single-celled, simple Amoeba evolved into a different, more complex molecule which then evolved into a different simple Life Form and changed and changed and changed, evolving finally into all the different species of Life that there are. This is taught as absolute Truth in every College and University in Western Civilization. Now let's expose this falsehood—In the whole record of Science—there is no Evidence—**None** of one species evolving into another Species (changes only occur within Species).

All fields of Science are to be supported and . . . honored. Scientism, however, is not Science! It is not Fact. It is Faith —in beliefs that are unsupported by Facts and Evidence; it gives a black eye to Science itself. The Man of Science, who believes in Scientism, worships his God everyday . . . by looking in the mirror.

The opinions of Scientists are no more credible than the weight of their Evidence . . . which is non-existent; it cannot be as it doesn't fit the criteria of Scientific proof. Theirs is a Belief system, not proof.

The Secular Humanist's belief in "No God" fails totally due to the fundamental Evidence of: 1) Human Nature,

2) <u>Culture</u>, and 3) <u>Intelligent Believers</u> in a Transcendent God.

1. <u>Human Nature–Human beings intuitively know good from bad; it's in their very Being.</u>

2. <u>All Cultures in history (thousands of years) believe (d) that there are Gods, or a God, outside and above Man. Every Clan, Tribe or Society from the dawn of Mankind has worshipped Gods. The earliest Civilizations in Egypt, Mesopotamia, China, India and the America's believed in Gods and an Afterlife.</u>

   <u>Belief in God(s) and Spirits is totally Universal— Barbarians, Muslims, Hindus, Buddhists, Mayans, Incas, Vikings and all other groups of Human Beings, without exception, believed in Beings who are not Human. This has existed as a Fact in all places and in all time, since time immemorial.</u>

3. <u>For over 4,000 years, outstanding men of great intelligence have used their intellects to reason to God (Thomas Aquinas is an example). People of modest intellect believe in God by looking up at the stars; they see the Edge of Infinity and believe in God.</u>

Chapter #9

Christianity

"God sent His Son to die—this is believable because it is absurd. He was buried and then rose again—this is certain because it is impossible."

—Tertullian, 2nd Century

There is a widespread belief in the West that all religions are the same; that one is "as good" as the other. It is a fact that there is a common Morality that all the great Religions of the world share. However, the Monotheistic Religions worship only one God. Christianity differs from all other religions and also from Judaism and Islam; it is unique.

Christians believe that: 1) God created the Universe, created the World, created Man and all living things, and 2) Man has a wounded Nature after Adam and Eve were expelled from the Garden of Eden. Mankind now knew evil as well as good and . . . sin entered the world. There was only one remedy: God in His infinite love became Man and assumed the entire burden of all of Mankind's sins. Christians believe that this was the great sacrifice performed by Christ. If we accept Christ's sacrifice on the basis of Faith, we will inherit God's gift of salvation. That is the essence of Christianity.

The so-called "Enlightenment" in the 17th Century was an epic time of rebellion against God. It was a time that gave birth to Secular Humanism—a belief that there is no God. Blaise Pascal—a Mathematical genius (he invented the first computer) and a Philosopher—was a rebel against the "no God" belief. He was the first modern Christian. This is what he wrote—"Man is capable of noble and wonderful thoughts and deeds, yet he also plots and performs horrible actions that are unworthy of even the lowest animals." Part of Man's greatness is that he can use his faculty of reason to recognize his baseness. Man has very high standards, but he is constantly falling short of them. He knows what is good, but at times he will not do it. He is subject to selfish and sinful desires. Often he gives in to those desires.

Blaise Pascal is renowned for his most famous "Pensee"—"The Wager." Simply stated, the "Wager" is this: either God exists or He does not. You can bet (Wager) two ways: You can bet–there is a God or you can bet—there is no God.

Bet #1 (by Believers): You bet there is a God:
> If God exists–you win. (Eternity)
> If God does not exist–you lose. (Nothing)

Bet #2 (by Atheists):   You bet there is no God:
> If God does not exist–you win. (Nothing)
> If God does exist–you lose. (Eternity)

Every Human Being must bet. (To refuse to bet is the same as betting that there is no God).

Pascal says, "Bet #1 is the wisest wager in the world and Bet #2 is the stupidest." Why? If God does exist, the Believer gains Heaven. The

Non-Believer is a person who doesn't even try to find the Truth; he sets his own rules/priorities and worships himself, not God—"My will be done" not "Thy will be done." As a result, he gets what he bargains for. He has now made his own destiny . . . for all eternity.

The propensity to sin is in Man's Nature. Selfishness, acquisitiveness, lust and greed are part of who we are as Humans. Sin structures our personalities, defines our thoughts and behavior. Sin can turn into a habit and then we sin routinely, almost unthinkingly.

The <u>only</u> truly meaningful, noble, uplifting, optimistic and joyful opportunity for Eternal Life for each individual Human Being is belief in God through our Redeemer, Jesus Christ. I say "opportunity" because Faith is a gift. It can be accepted or rejected; intentionally or <u>negligently</u>.

Heaven is God's domain, where He is eternally present. Hell is where God is eternally absent. God doesn't reject the Atheist; the Atheist rejects God. God doesn't dispatch the Atheist to Hell; the Atheist wishes to close his eyes and heart to God, and God reluctantly grants him his wish. The gates of Hell are locked from the inside.

Christianity

Truth:

Each man seeks to know; he seeks information. From this information, a man makes decisions and forms opinions which then become his Beliefs. They are, however, his personal Beliefs. Whether his Beliefs are in conformity with the Facts, the Truth, the Reality, is another matter entirely. Objective reality trumps opinion every time, if personal opinion is not in agreement with objective Reality (i.e., the Truth of the matter); this is true regardless of whether that personal opinion is held by one person or millions of persons. Personal Beliefs may or may not be true. Examples: Jack Peters believes he is Napoleon; Ed Blakeley believes the earth is flat and the sun goes around the earth; Julia Snell believes Man never walked on the moon . . . well, they truly do believe it but their Personal Beliefs are not true. The Objective Reality is the Truth; the Evidence proves the Truth and Facts are Facts.

Faith is inextricably tied up with, "Personhood." From the moment we are conceived, we are related to our Mother. For the rest of our lives, we have relationships with the other Persons we meet in our lives. We learn to rely on some and avoid others. Those we trust, we rely on; we have Faith in them. Experience tells us they can be trusted. Not just those we know who have proven themselves reliable but even those we don't know: when getting into an airplane or an elevator; eating food prepared by someone else; driving at 55mph on one side of the road with another driver going the same speed in the other direction. Faith is a reality of every person's life, every bit as much as Reason. Faith and Reason together are essential to every person's life. The question, the fundamental question is—Faith in what? Is our Faith grounded in experience? Is it grounded in Reason? Is our Faith solidly grounded whether that Faith is in things, people or God? The answer to these questions should determine how you should live your Life while here on Earth.

Many people, baptized or not, say they believe in God, (Big deal! The Devil believes in God!) They make up a nice, benign, Grandfatherly old guy. A silly-putty God who can be molded to each person's fancy. These spiritual Walter Mitty's make up an imaginary God that exists only in that person's imagination. It is a fantasy of the Mind; nothing more.

We, each of us, spend thousands of hours learning. Learning history, arithmetic, higher math, language, sports, art, a trade, a profession. Yet we spend almost <u>no time</u> learning how to grow Spiritually. There once was a Little Pig who worked so hard to build . . . a house of straw!

<u>What happens if we ignore things Spiritual</u>? We <u>choose</u> to remain ignorant so as to not interfere with what we want to do. We satisfy our desires and appetites in junk food for body and mind and then what happens? If we don't exercise: 1) <u>Physically</u>—we become slobs; 2) <u>Mentally</u>—we remain ignorant; 3) <u>Emotionally</u>—we become basket cases; 4) <u>Spiritually</u>—we ignore Life and Death Questions; we become easy prey for Satan through the Seven Deadly Sins—Pride, Lust, Avarice, Envy, Anger, Gluttony and Sloth. Every one of us has experienced this in our own life.

On Judgment Day, "I didn't know" just isn't going to wash when the failure is due to laziness, a bad conscience, refusal to accept and believe because it might interfere with what we want to do. It is clear that you get out of life what you put into it. Isn't it obvious that this will apply to your Spiritual life as well?

What do you believe is going to happen to you when you die? What you believe is the basis of what you do, or not do. How you act and live your life results in your Destiny. In truth, you, yourself, chose what happens to you after your earthly life ends by your decisions and actions during your life. Death–for some of us it comes sooner than later but it does inexorably come. A wise man once said, "You should live you life 'as if' it was your last day on earth; you're sure to be a better person." Death is the termination of mortality. The Soul and Spirit move into Eternity. You should ask yourself these vital questions: What do I believe? What happens when I die? Do I believe the promises of Jesus? Am I committed to saving my Soul for Heaven and not Hell? Remember this–what you do in this life determines where your Soul will be for all Eternity. It is your choice–choose Heaven, not Hell.

What is the meaning of Life? Life is either purposeful or it is not. Structured or chaotic. People are afraid of dying; this is natural. However, it's not a question of "whether", only a question of "when." It is monumentally foolish/stupid not to think about it as it most certainly is going to happen–to you, to me, to all of us.

Walker Percy, the novelist, writes about life: "This life is too much trouble, far too strange, to arrive at the end of it and being asked what you made of your life and then answer–'Not very much.' That just won't do! A poor show! Life is a mystery, Love a delight. Therefore, I take it as axiomatic, that one should settle for nothing less than the infinite mystery, and the infinite delight, that is God."

Christianity

Wisdom:

Every Human Being accumulates information and knowledge. <u>Wisdom</u>, however, exists only in some persons. The Ancient Philosophers taught that <u>Wisdom</u> was life's highest and best goal and end. Socrates taught that the beginning of Wisdom is to seek it. History proves over and over again in each age that a man may be learned–a Scientist, a Mathematician, a Philosopher, a Scholar but . . . still not wise.

The author, Tolstoy, summarizes it best in his monumental book, *War and Peace*:

> "'<u>All we can know is that we know nothing</u>. And that's the height of <u>human wisdom</u> . . . the highest wisdom is not founded on reason alone, nor on those worldly Sciences of Physics, Chemistry, and the like, into which intellectual knowledge is divided.' <u>The highest wisdom</u> is '<u>but one Science–the Science of the Whole–the Science which explains the whole Creation and Man's place in it</u>. To receive that Science, it is necessary to purify and renew one's inner self . . . <u>And to attain this end</u>, we have the <u>light called Conscience</u> that God <u>has implanted</u> in our souls.'"

Aristotle differentiates Wisdom from the other Sciences which deal with principles and causes and proofs thereof. Wisdom is the Queen of Sciences (he calls it, "The Divine Science") as it concerns itself with "First Things"–the first principle and cause of life itself. Aquinas states this also and takes it a monumental step further. How? By showing that

Faith and Reason are resolved in Jesus Christ. God becomes Man. Our Creator becomes our Savior in history.

Aquinas identifies three types of Wisdom counterfeits:

1. Man seeks as his highest good–earthly things–<u>Earthly Wisdom</u>.
2. Man seeks as his highest good–sensual things–<u>Sensual Wisdom</u>.
3. Man seeks as his highest good–intellectual excellence–<u>Devilish Wisdom</u> which is Pride.

True and authentic Wisdom not only contemplates God and Divine things but also directs man's thoughts and actions to moral action in this life.

"To have Wisdom is to love wisely." (Spinoza) "What you love, you desire." What do <u>you</u> desire? Wonder is the beginning of natural wisdom which Aristotle regarded as the ultimate goal of human inquiry.

Wisdom is an act of the Intellect. Charity (Love) is an act of the will.

<u>Two Wolves</u>

One evening an old Cherokee told his grandson about a battle that goes on inside people. He said, "My son, the battle is between 'two wolves' inside us all.

One wolf is Evil. It is anger, envy, sorrow, regret, greed, arrogance, self-pity, guilt, resentment, inferiority, lies, false pride, superiority and ego.

The other wolf is Good. It is joy, peace, love, hope, serenity, humility, kindness, benevolence, empathy, generosity, truth, compassion and faith."

The grandson thought about it for a minute and then asked his grandfather, "Which wolf wins?"

The old Cherokee simply replied, "The one you feed."

Now this is old Indian wisdom.

<u>Christianity</u>

<u>Credo:</u>

<u>This is the "Credo"</u> of Catholics; it is what we believe: We believe in Jesus Christ; the New and Old Testament. We believe God created Man in His own image–as a thinking Being with Free Will. We believe He gave us laws of right conduct, admonitions and rules regarding wrong conduct so as to guide and help us achieve perfection and eternal life. We believe in the Theological Virtues—Faith, Hope and Love—and pray daily for an increase in Faith, an increase in Hope and most of all, an increase in Love—a giving of self first to God and then to our fellow men as God's creatures.

We believe we are answerable to our Creator for all we have done and how we made use of the gifts/talents He has given us. We believe our Faith is illumined by reason and certified by our Conscience. We believe that with God's grace, given and poured out by the Holy Spirit, that we shall see God face-to-face once the soul has been purified and is without the stain of all sin.

The Catholic Faith is based on Faith and Revelation. It is a relationship with the three Persons of the Trinity—the Father, the Son and the Holy Spirit. The Catholic faith is based on Revelation in the Old and New Testaments. "The Eternal Word," Jesus Christ, is revealed in the New Testament; the Repository of that Word, unchanged for 2000 years, is in the Magisterium of the Catholic Church.

To save Mankind, God sent His <u>only Son</u> to redeem Mankind. On Christmas Day, the new "Adam" was born—God sent his Son, Jesus, as our Savior, to redeem Humanity by expiation for the Sins of Man. Christ was crucified for Mankind's sin—He is truly Mankind's Savior.

> God the Father is a Person.
> Jesus Christ is a Person.
> The Holy Spirit is a Person.

Three Persons—one God. **The Blessed Trinity** is a profound mystery. We have total confidence and assurance that it is true. Jesus Christ told his Disciples that **He was the Way, the Truth and the Life**. He identified God as His Father and Himself as His Son and, before His ascension into Heaven, told His Disciples that He was sending them the Holy Spirit and He did.

Christianity

A Foretaste of Eternity: Christianity Can Change Your Life

"Finally it is not a matter of obedience. Finally it is a matter of love."

-Thomas Moore, *A Man for All Seasons*

Christianity is an embrace of a Person—that Person is Jesus Christ. Christ is the most influential figure in history. Christ is the only person in history who formed a whole Religion totally around his own Person. The Christ we encounter in the New Testament is extraordinary. We know Christ as we know Socrates, through the reports of others. We hear Christ's voice in the four Gospels, Matthew, Mark, Luke and John who were His Apostles. These men knew Christ, heard His message and commandment of loving God and Man and witnessed His Resurrection after He was crucified and they believed in Him, His teachings and His Commandments.

These first Apostles and Disciples witnessed Christ's resurrection. They testified to what they heard and what they saw–before and after His Crucifixion. Their cries of lamentation on His death on the Cross were replaced with cries of joy at His Resurrection. Proclaiming Christ crucified and Christ risen, they launched the greatest wave of religious conversion in history. The number of Christians increased from a few score at the time of Christ's death to around thirty million by the early fourth century. The early Christians did not hesitate to identify themselves with a man who had been branded a traitor and a criminal. They endured imprisonment, torture, exile, and death rather than renounce their faith in Christ and His Church. These conversions occurred in the teeth of fierce opposition and the persecution of the greatest empire in the ancient world, the empire of Rome.

The great events that defined his life are recorded in the New Testament. The earliest Gospels were composed within thirty years after Christ's death, and the last was written before 100 AD. "If Christ had not been raised," Paul writes in 1 Corinthians 15:17, "our preaching is useless and so is your faith." The Resurrection is the most important event in Christianity. The Gospel records 19 appearances of Christ after the Resurrection!

What can be said about Christ can also be said about Christianity. It matters. It is the very core and center of Western Civilization. Christianity's central claims about God and the nature of reality are supported by the greatest discoveries of modern Science and modern scholarship.

Christianity makes sense of who we are in the World. Each of us needs a framework in which to understand Reality. It is a World View that makes things fit together. Science and Reason were seamlessly integrated in a Christian beginning, because modern Science was founded on a 1500-year Christian framework. Christianity has always embraced both Reason and Faith. Reason helps us to discover things from experience; Faith helps us discover things that transcend experience. Christianity provides a comprehensive and believable account of who Human Beings are and why we are here.

Religion is the formal activity we use to connect with the source of all good—God. The Catholic Church is our Religion; it states our Creed in the "Catechism of the Catholic Church". It states that: Jesus is the Way, the Truth and the Life. He told that to His Apostles and His Disciples. He established His Church to help us find the Way, find the Truth and gain Eternal Life. The Catholic Church is the constant beacon we have to navigate on the ocean of life and bring us to safe harbor.

Christianity infuses life with a powerful and exhilarating sense of purpose. Atheism in most of its current forms posits a Universe without meaning. Christianity makes life a moral drama in which we play a starring role. Contrary to what secular critics say, the Christian does not and cannot hold our life on earth to be unimportant. Indeed, it is of the highest importance. The reason is obvious: it is this life that determines our status in the next life. Our fate for eternity hinges on how we live now. Life in this world is a way to live a life with meaning and purpose.

Christianity proclaims our destiny is to be with God. Our fundamental relationship is with Him. Only the Supernatural can finally produce enduring joy in the face of life's tragedies. Funerals remind us of our own death and the realization that we are mortal and will die. How I live; what I believe shapes and determines my destiny when I die.

Realizing this, we need to raise the level of our personal lives, bringing conscience into harmony with the way we live. Christianity gives us reasons to follow our Conscience; it is not simply our innermost desire but the voice of God speaking through us. Virtue is God's stamp in our hearts. We will be good not because we have to but because we want to; it is our free choice.

The desire for Truth is part of our Human Nature. Jesus Christ, the Eternal Word (of God) is Truth itself—not an abstract idea but a Person that is Reality itself. The pivotal/bedrock of our Faith is a relationship.

The relationship with Christ is a love affair between God and Man. The Love of the Creator is a gift to us. We creatures can accept or reject this gift. We have Free Will.

Ultimately we are called not only to happiness and goodness but also to holiness. What counts for God is not only our external conduct but also our inward disposition. Holiness is not something we do for God. It is something we do with God. In a society based on self-fulfillment and self-esteem, Christ calls us to a heroic task.

We can decide; we can choose to act and follow God's Law or follow perversions of that Law where Faith becomes "Justice." "Justice" becomes "Ideology" and "Ideology" becomes the exclusive Will of Human Beings. In this perversion—it's not, "Thy will be done," but my Will (Human) be done—the "No God" credo.

What we believe is of fundamental importance as to how we live our lives as mortal Human Beings; which in turn will affect and effect where our Souls are for all Eternity.

Here is an extraordinary profession of Faith; a "Credo" of Truth, Beauty and Goodness by Monsignor Lorenzo Albacete, entitled—"**Because of My Name**."

"It is not enough to say that Jesus Christ teaches us the Truth about human life. The Christian faith affirms much more. The Truth of life is the Mystery at the origin of all that exists. All religions seek to discover this Truth. Only the Christian, however, will affirm that the Truth became a human being in the womb of a Jewish woman; that he was born as a baby and grew up as a man; that he was

followed by people who were struck by the way he lived his life; and that he was executed by some of his opponents but he rose from the dead victorious over space and time and is thus still present in his humanity in our midst. Only a Christian would say this. Jesus is the name of a concrete individual man who is the human embodiment of the Truth that all religions seek. He is the Truth made man. This is what we believe. It is not enough to say that Jesus is the name we give to the Truth. Jesus is the man who is the incarnation of the Truth. For this reason, before identifying himself as the Truth, Jesus calls himself the Way. Jesus is the Way to the Truth. To be a Christian is to embrace the Way to the Truth that Jesus is . . . We do not seek solutions to the problems of life derived from religious sentiments, spiritual approaches, or philosophical convictions. We do not have answers to questions. In each circumstance of life, whatever it is, we seek not an answer but a Presence, the human presence that is the way to the "Answer," to the Truth. We do not come together as Church to find intellectual answers to our questions about the meaning and purpose of life. This is to reduce the Church to an ideology. We come together not to find answers but to learn how to recognize and affirm a Presence. The Church is not "our way" of finding answers to our religious quest for the Truth; it is the method through which the Truth becomes incarnate for us . . . We come together as the Church to learn how to recognize the fact of this Presence, and to witness to it in any circumstance of life, especially when there are no answers. Jesus Christ is the way to the Answer. In him, way and answer coincide."

Epilogue

Two friends, Mr. Able and Mr. Baker, by name, book a cruise on a luxury liner. First Class. Excellent accommodations, superb food, and exceptional wines. And . . . best of all, no interruptions as they play chess, discuss politics, religion, humanity—its past, present and future, and social and economic issues. They have been doing this for years; enjoying each other's company and swordplay. They admire each other's talents in argumentation, polemics and apologetics, and savor the excellent clash of ideas and beliefs.

They rarely agreed on anything, however, not to be contrarians, heaven forbid! They knew each other as smart, learned, reasonable and knowledgeable torchbearers for the good of humanity, society (in all its aspects) and the human condition. They never yelled or fumed; their arguments were passionate (they really believed in what they were saying) but never pejorative. Well, almost never, unless politics was the topic and then occasionally in the heat of battle, an insult would pop up and a like insult returned. Glares, embarrassment at the lapse in protocol, and, then a return to proper reasoned discourse. Here were two "Enlightened Gentlemen." Mr. Able was a devout Catholic and a Thomistic Scholar who lived his "Credo" (see below). Mr. Baker was a devout Secular Humanist who taught Philosophy and Social Ethics at Harvard University who lived his beliefs. The two always went at it lustily with their usual thrusts and parries in the swordplay. As you might suspect, neither ever convinced the other of anything but enjoy they did their verbal combat.

They got on the great ship along with 2,220 other passengers. That afternoon the majestic ship cast off its hawsers amid cheers, flag waving and booming blasts of the vessel's horns and headed out into the Atlantic. At dinner that night, the two friends recollected all the stimulating debates they had had over the years. They dined and wined well; totally enjoying each other's company. Over cigars and port they agreed to meet next morning at 8:00am and get down to serious business. That night, April 12th, the great ship sailed on over smooth, calm seas. At breakfast the next day the first thing they did was agree to each develop a list of Topics (numbered #1 thru #10) which they would then discuss in turn with the first Topic decided by a flip of the coin.

So the first full day at sea, April 13th, was spent by the two in deep reflection and much thought in drawing up their respective list of Topics. Meanwhile, the 2,218 other passengers strolled the decks, swam in the pool, played shuffleboard and enjoyed carefree "happy times." These fellow passengers were enjoying the cruise oblivious to the intense thought processes and concerns of our two "Enlightened Gentlemen." That night, at the cocktail hour, the two enjoyed their usual libations—a scotch and soda for Mr. Able and a glass of wine for Mr. Baker—and exchanged their lists. Surprisingly both listed as Topic #1–"What is the meaning of life?" This topic was to be discussed next morning, the second full day at sea.

Next morning, however, neither Mr. Baker nor Mr. Able were feeling well, so they agreed to forgo any discussion that day so that they would be in top form for their first topic the next day. Alas, it was not to be. At 11:40 pm that night, April 14, 1912, the Titanic, captained by Edward Smith, hit an iceberg and sank in icy waters. 1,511 passengers died that night, as did Mr. Able and Mr. Baker. Their drowning in the icy waters stilled the sound and fury of their able arguments.

At 3am, April 15th, 1914, Mr. Able, Mr. Baker and 1511 other persons died in the icy waters of the North Atlantic. What happened to them thereafter? Good Question! The ultimate reality of whether God exists and there is Life after Death are not dependent upon what Mr. Able or Mr. Baker thought or believed. The Objective Fact, the Reality, the Truth is that there either is or isn't a God. There is or isn't life after Death.

Therefore:

1. If Mr. Baker is correct, 1513 people died. Finale. End of Life. Oblivion.
2. If Mr. Able is correct, 1513 people died and they will answer to their Creator for the lives they have lived. If Mr. Able lived his "Credo" he lives on; for all Eternity in a state of happiness, joy and union with God. As for Mr. Baker, it would seem from reading the New Testament that his fate will be quite different. As for the other 1511 souls? Who knows? God only knows and He is not telling you and me directly.

*   *   *

Mr. Able's Credo

I believe God created me in His own image—a thinking Human Being with Free Will; an Embodied Soul. I believe He gave us laws of right conduct and admonitions and laws regarding wrong conduct. I believe He sent His word, Jesus Christ, into the World to redeem fallen Man and expiate Humanity's sin—mine and all other Human Beings. I believe that the Bible, both the Old and New Testament, is the true word of God speaking to each one of us.

I believe in the theological virtues—Faith, Hope and Love—and give daily thanks for the gifts and talents He has given me. I believe my Faith is illuminated by reason and certified by my conscience. I believe that with God's grace, given and poured out by the Holy Spirit, that I shall see God face-to-face once my soul has been purified and is without blemish—a perfect Human Being, a Son of God.

Author's Note:
Dear Reader,
I hope this book helps you on your life's journey and that you arrive safely at your Final Destination.

A Fellow Pilgrim,

Jim Barrett